10 04063
KU-161-014

THE WIVES OF DOWNING STREET

The Wives of Downing Street

KIRSTY McLEOD

COLLINS
St James's Place, London
1976

William Collins Sons & Co Ltd
London · Glasgow · Sydney · Auckland
Toronto · Johannesburg

First published August 1976
Reprinted October 1976

ISBN 0 00 211953 6

Set in Garamond
Made and Printed in Great Britain by
William Collins Sons & Co Ltd Glasgow

For my mother and father

'What wickedness and what folly to undervalue and be insensible to the affection of a wife.'

Sir Robert Peel

Contents

Illustrations

Acknowledgements

As a newcomer to the field of historical biography, I owe an enormous debt to a number of eminent experts who have taken the time and trouble to read and comment on my typescript. For their immensely valuable and generous advice I have to thank Stanley Ayling, biographer of Chatham; Professor Norman Gash, who read my chapter on Lady Peel; John Prest, himself an author of a definitive biography of Lord John Russell; Professor Michael Foot, editor of The Gladstone Diaries, and John Grigg whose first book on Lloyd George I so greatly enjoyed and whose second I look forward to with pleasure. While I am pleased to acknowledge my debt to them, the responsibility for any blunders is entirely my own.

My thanks are also due to the members of the Lloyd George and Asquith families who have helped me by suggesting reading matter, tracing photographs and talking to me about their own very personal memories. Earl Lloyd George was unfailingly helpful over the chapter on his grandmother. Baroness Elliot of Harwood was interesting and enlightening about her sister, Mrs Asquith. Mrs Raymond Asquith talked to me at length in Somerset and Mark Bonham-Carter was also kind enough to read this chapter and make most valuable suggestions.

Among the long-suffering members of my own family,

Acknowledgements

I owe especial thanks to Sibbald and Robin McMichen for putting up with a somewhat overprolonged stay; thanks also to Christopher Hudson for his much-needed criticism of the text.

The Role of the Political Wife

The prejudice against women in politics has until recently been as strong as the prejudice against women in the Church. Reading the textbook histories of Britain, one might suppose that Downing Street was an entirely masculine retreat with no more of a female presence in it than was required to sweep up the cigar ash and clean the brandy glasses. But in the last two decades, a number of political women have come to the fore, one of them to the highest position achieved by a woman in British parliamentary history. They have shown as much energy, determination and political shrewdness as any of their male colleagues. With their example in mind, it should be possible to look more clear-sightedly at the role of political wives who, over the last two hundred years, have exhibited the same skill and resolution behind the scenes – in influencing their husbands or their husbands' colleagues and, through them, the course of British political history.

Different aspects of this role can be seen in the accounts that follow of the wives of prime ministers from the elder Pitt to Henry Asquith. I have chosen eight: the eight who seemed to me to complement each other best. Lady Peel and Mary Anne Disraeli are perhaps the most conventionally supportive, but no less important for being so. Mary Anne gave Disraeli the opportunity to start in politics; Julia Peel gave her husband, Robert, a reason for continuing. Lady Chatham so far exceeded the bounds of marital obligation that, with her help, Lord Chatham was able to continue in office, though seriously ill. At the other end of the scale, both Lady Palmerston and Lady John Russell wielded considerable political as well as personal influence, while Catherine Gladstone was responsible for prolonging her husband's tenure of office for several years. Margot Asquith merited inclusion for her own remarkable personality and because she brought the wind of change of the twentieth century into Downing Street. Finally, there is Margaret Lloyd George, in her own way the most independent of all the wives and surely the only one who could have enjoyed political acclaim in her own right.

These then are the eight, but there are many more I could have chosen. Lady Salisbury, for instance, whose husband early in his career wrote candidly in his diary: 'I have come to the conclusion that I shall probably do Parliament well if I do marry, and that I shall certainly make nothing of it if I do not.' Unworldly and retiring by nature, he married a forceful, ambitious wife, who gave a sense of purpose to his aspirations, urging him on 'to play the great game' of politics whenever his resolution flagged. Lady Salisbury guarded her husband's health devotedly, making sure that he prepared himself for his political work with plenty of exercise and sleep. Like Lord John Russell's wife, she organized her calendar around her husband's activities: Sundays she set aside for him as a day of peace and privacy, when he could walk in his grounds undisturbed or retire to his library to read and contemplate. The House of Commons rose early on Wednesdays, and she chose that day to entertain guests at their house in Arlington Street. These soirées and her lavish garden parties at Hatfield were well attended, even outside the Tory party. They gave Lady Salisbury the chance to appeal to uncommitted new MPs through their wives. On other days, when the House was sitting late, she could be seen in the Ladies' Gallery in the early hours of the morning, waiting to snatch some time with her husband on his walk home across St James's Park. Often it was dawn before they could set out together.

It is not by accident that qualities of selflessness and determination are evident in all these women to a striking degree. It is probably true to say that women are not drawn to marry men of action and decision unless they are prepared to make some sacrifices. They know they are marrying men whose work – be it politics or motor-racing – is an absorbing passion. Their rewards are many and various, but they are not those of a comfort-loving housewife. Of the prime ministers' wives I write about, possibly only Margaret Lloyd George could not have had a shrewd idea of what lay in store for her. It is interesting to note that Margaret Lloyd George was the one wife to rebel, and leave her husband's side to go and live in Wales.

Sometimes, of course, they were asked to make sacrifices beyond anything they could have prepared for. Lord Chatham's mental illness provoked the severest test of his wife's loyalty and courage. Hester Chatham, the provident daughter of a rich family, allowed her inheritance to be squandered and her children's future put in jeopardy in order to provide for her husband's megalomaniac fantasies. Totally alone, she bore the brunt of his madness, staving off creditors and arranging loans so that his extravagant whims could be satisfied and he could be left in peace.

Without Hester, Chatham's political life would have been cut short. Without Mary Anne, Disraeli's might well never have flourished. It must have seemed to their contemporaries the oddest of relationships, this between Disraeli and the sharp, birdlike, unglamorous older woman for whom he felt at first a teasing affection, then admiration, and, finally, a lasting love. Even before they knew each other well, Mary Anne adopted Disraeli as her 'political pet'. She canvassed indefatigably to secure his election, wearing the Tory colours made up into a special election dress. Later it was she who enabled him to concentrate on a political career by bailing him out of his considerable debts. At one point he had been afraid to go out to dine for fear of being 'nabbed'. She spent £40,000 on one election campaign alone, and it was in no small measure due to her that Disraeli, 'that damned bumptious Jew boy', succeeded to the highest office in the land, for which in the past the prerequisite had been a title or a fortune or preferably both together. Before Mary Anne became his wife, Disraeli bemoaned his lot in *Vivian Grey*: 'Were I the son of a millionaire, or a noble I might have *all*.' Later in life, his financial worries behind him, he could afford to be more light-hearted. 'Every woman should marry, and no man,' he is supposed to have said, thus cavalierly dismissing the role played by his wife in his career. Mary Anne's reply to this is not recorded. What we do know is that she was as selfless as any of the others in her attentions to him. For some all-night sittings she would order a cold supper and a brougham, in which she and Disraeli would picnic between division bells. On other occasions she would sit up until the early hours at home, waiting for him to return. 'I always have a hot supper for him when he comes home, and lights, lights, plenty of lights; Dizzy always likes lights. And then he tells me everything that has happened in the House, and then I clap him off to bed.'

Domestic economy aside, the influence of political wives is naturally regulated by the conventions within which they are allowed to exercise it. Of all these women, there cannot be much doubt that Viscount Palmerston's wife, Emily, had the most direct influence on affairs of state. Brought up in political circles, she had benefited from the custom in the Whig party of her day for great ladies of fashion to be taken into the confidence of many leading statesmen. By the time she married Palmerston, Emily had as much inside knowledge as her husband and, within the Whig party at least, many more contacts. It was natural for her to employ what Henry Asquith called 'the technique of the *salon*', which, he said, 'made her an active and most efficient co-partner in Palmerston's fortunes.'

The technique of the salon. It was a social weapon which its adversaries underestimated at their peril. In this country it was a significant instrument of Liberal and Conservative politics throughout the nineteenth century and even – if Margot Asquith's eclectic and highly individual mode of entertaining can be called a salon – into the twentieth. We may suppose that Lady Palmerston's drawing-room witnessed much the same sort of salon politics as we read about in the novels of Disraeli and Trollope – a deceptively silken web of flattery, malice and intrigue which often appealed as much to opponents of Palmerston's policies as to supporters of them. At the centre of this web, Lady Palmerston acted as her husband's political manager and confidante throughout the most prominent and distinguished part of his career.

It is indicative of the active role she played that Emily Palmerston almost alone among the prime ministers' wives in this 150-year span from Chatham to Lloyd George, was content to see her husband relinquish his high office. At the age of sixty-eight, after a lifetime spent in politics, she declared, 'I would rather my husband was only Foreign Minister or Home Secretary, for since he became Prime Minister I see nothing of him. He never comes to bed till four or five o'clock.' But she was the exception. Many women who had spent their lives sacrificing their own interests to further their husbands' careers were unwilling to see what they had striven for obliterated in the tide of political fortune. The wives of Robert Peel and, in this century, Henry Campbell-Bannerman, gentle and unassuming ladies both, wielded their greatest influence in persuading their husbands not to relinquish their positions of power. Were it not for Julia, Peel used to say, he would long since have retired from politics. And after the 1905 Conservative election defeat when Sir Henry Campbell-Bannerman was under pressure from some of his colleagues to retire from the leadership of the Liberal party, it was his frail and sickly wife who urged him, against his first judgement, to form an administration. 'No surrender!' he is supposed to have said when he came back to the conference table after discussing his future with her.

Historically the most significant of these is the case of Catherine Gladstone. A woman of determination and strength of character to match Gladstone's own, she encouraged him to stay in power long after his failing health indicated that he should resign and leave the way open to a younger man. For one thing, she was determined to force through a Home Rule bill for Ireland, so that her nephew, Frederick Cavendish, Chief Secretary for Ireland when he was assassinated in 1882, should not have died in vain. More than this, her loyalty to her husband was such that she believed right to the end that there was no one worthy to step into his shoes. Gladstone understood this and accepted it. He made a telling remark to Margot Asquith before her marriage in 1894. 'You have a great and noble work to perform. May strength be abundantly granted you.'

No doubt Margot appreciated his blessing. But times

had changed when her husband achieved Gladstone's old office. Like Lady Palmerston, Margot Asquith had friends on both sides of the House. But she was able to exercise her influence directly on an admiring circle of bright, young Liberal MPs for whom she was the most witty and talented hostess in London. She was even able to suggest political appointments to Arthur Balfour, her lifelong friend who became Tory Prime Minister. Alfred Milner was appointed Chairman of the Board of Inland Revenue on her recommendation.

With Margot Asquith, the time had come when a woman of determination and character could achieve political ends to some extent independently of her husband. It was an evolution, not a radical change. Both Margot Asquith and Margaret Lloyd George were adamantly against the 1918 enfranchisement bill, even though it gave the vote only to householders and the wives of householders over the age of thirty. Both of them abhorred the suffragette movement and were satisfied to promote the rights of women, such as they saw them, through established constitutional methods. It was all right, for example, for Margaret Lloyd George to discuss maternity benefits with Queen Mary – and then to whisper a discreet word in her husband's ear; but it was not all right for suffragettes to challenge the status quo. Indeed, Margot Asquith's step-children even threw things with impunity at the women chained beneath the Downing Street windows.

Yet there can be no doubt that their relative independence gave both these last two women a more complex idea of where their duty lay. When Asquith fell from power, his wife felt it incumbent upon her to go to work in order to salvage his career. Margot was already in her late fifties but nevertheless set about writing books, dashed off articles and embarked on gruelling lecture tours so that her husband could be freed from financial pressures while he tried to make a come-back into politics.

Her loyalty was to her husband. It was also to herself. We get the same feeling listening to the testimony of Margaret Lloyd George when she had to appear in court on behalf of her husband during a libel suit over another woman. She knew Lloyd George to be a philanderer; she was independent enough of him to make her own home in Wales. In protecting her husband's reputation it was her own life she was protecting, and that of her children.

The formation of the Primrose League and the Women's Liberal Foundation at the turn of the century, had made the open participation of women in politics respectable. Indeed, after the 1883 Corrupt Practices Act which had made paid canvassing at elections illegal, it became of paramount importance at an election campaign to have the help and support of a loyal woman. The enfranchisement of women after the First World War was the formal acknowledgement of this new 'public' participation. Whatever Margaret Lloyd George may have felt about the suffragettes, it is no coincidence that she was the first prime minister's wife to build up a following by speaking in public. She drew her political influence not from her husband but from the solid power base in Wales which she herself had built up, and which contributed so much to the Liberal party. From there it was a short step to women MPs in the House of Commons and women politicians in the seats of power which, until so recently, they could have approached only through their husbands.

Lady Chatham

In the summer of 1735, a young MP called William Pitt paid his first visit to the great house of Stowe in Buckinghamshire. The home of Viscount Cobham and seat of the mighty Grenville clan, it was open house to a select band of political dissidents and literati. Pitt soon found himself far removed from his own comparatively undistinguished family, walking the palatial grounds to view Congreve's monument, or hovering to hear Pope speak.

He can have had no illusions about why he had been asked there. He had been a schoolfriend of Cobham's nephew, George Lyttelton, and through him had come to know those other Cobham nephews, the five brothers Grenville, but they hardly moved in the same social circles. Nevertheless, politically all this Stowe House group was united in its common hatred of Sir Robert Walpole, the autocratic First Lord of the Treasury, who had ruled England since 1720 and is generally conceded to have been the country's first prime minister. Together Pitt and Cobham's 'cubs' formed a small but vociferous opposition faction, spearheaded by Pitt's brilliance as a public speaker.

So dazzled was he at belonging to this elite 'cousinhood' that he scarcely can have noticed the Grenvilles' young sister, Hester, at fourteen still in the schoolroom.

She noticed him. For nineteen years she was his devoted admirer and friend, treasuring his briefest notes and badgering his friends for news of him. She seems to have sensed the greatness in him even then. But to him she was still a child and he was on the threshold of his career, a tall, slender, richly-dressed young man with flashing eyes and a great beaked nose. Nothing would have amazed him more than the thought that, after half a lifetime of bachelordom, he should suddenly, in gouty middle-age, fall passionately in love. He was forty-six and Hester thirty-three when they finally decided to marry.

In her portraits Hester Grenville has all the characteristics of her haughty family, with her well-bred, bony face and elegantly tip-tilted Grenville nose. In reality, she seems to have been a practical, sensible girl, brought up without fuss in the country despite the splendour of her background. In the first place, her own immediate family were very much the junior branch of the Grenvilles until Hester's uncle, Cobham, died in 1749, leaving her mother his heir. Mrs Grenville became a Viscountess but Hester at twenty-six was still Miss Grenville and might have remained so, had it not been for her ambitious brother. Richard Temple-Grenville, as he soon styled himself, felt that only an earldom was good enough for his family. He did not rest until his mother was created Countess Temple.

Most of Hester's childhood was spent in the friendly and comparatively relaxed household at Wotton, although at times she exchanged this for the grander formality of Stowe. Her interests were those of any country child. With her five brothers she loved to ride and explore the surrounding countryside. She could keep up with any of them, even when it came to climbing hills. In their different ways they all took an affectionate and proprietary interest in her: priggish George delivered pointed moral lectures; Richard, the eldest, later Earl Temple, treated her with clumsy bonhomie. But it was the middle brother, James, who grew up closest to her, and when she came of age, vetted every prospective romance.

For although she married late, Hester was never short of suitors. What she lacked in beauty or wit, she made up for by being immensely rich. Her pleasant, wholesome country life had left her serene and even-tempered. She had a tall, graceful figure set off by rich auburn hair. So it was no surprise that when she was twenty-one, her brother Thomas complained of not having heard from her, adding, 'If it is your Lovers, I excuse you but upon no other accounts.' Three years later, James wrote, championing the cause of one particular suitor, Simon Truelove. 'It is impossible to look for a more advantageous proposal,' he began, and then, half-teasing, half in earnest for after all, Hester was now twenty-four: 'My dear, Meg, you grow old and it is time for you to think of a decent retirement from business.'

From all accounts Hester was thinking of anything but this. Despite his name, Mr Truelove disappeared without trace and Hester was next seen with the 'charming, spirited' Captain Geary. Together they excited comment in the staid resort of Tunbridge Wells by riding around at all hours, and, worst crime of all in a spa, breakfasting before they drank the waters. 'I am told wonders of your horsemanship,' fumed George, 'but seriously ten miles an hour is rather too much . . .' Fortunately for George's peace of mind, Captain Geary was not long in favour. Nor was Richard Berenger, Hester's cousin, who shared her great love of horses. 'She has used him cheaply,' commented Elizabeth Wyndham, Hester's future sister-in-law and friend. It was a fair comment, although not a reflection on Hester's character, for she was by nature straightforward, kind and loyal. Nevertheless, she was a Grenville and had a fund of cool reserve which she brought into play when her affections were not engaged.

But of course they were engaged, and engaged elsewhere, and possibly it was sheer frustration that accounted for her mood. Certainly, her closest friends guessed that her real feelings were for Pitt. On her betrothal, one of them, Jane Hamilton, wrote: 'I will burn my books if you are not happy together, but as you will remember I long ago gave you to him.' Hester gave herself too, by word and deed over the years. She sent endless enquiries after his health and cherished his rushed replies. She offered him her London house immediately he decided to stay in town. All her actions suggest that she was desperately in love.

And after all there can be no other reason why a woman of her unruffled common sense should suddenly, after nineteen years, decide to marry within the space of two short weeks. For Pitt, with his flamboyant, mercurial nature, such a decisive step must have seemed natural enough. But it is unlikely that he realized until quite late the depth of Hester's feelings.

Not that Pitt was allowed to remain insensible to feminine charm. On the contrary, his rich clothes and courtly manner made him a general favourite. Mrs Montagu's sister, Sarah, sighed for him. Hester's cousin, Molly West, actively pursued him until she gave up in despair and settled for the future Admiral Alexander Hood. He was a delightful, witty companion and a popular guest at the houses of his friends. But always he held himself aloof. Only in 1754 when his political hopes had been shattered and his confidence undermined did he unbend enough to allow Hester, a proven friend, into his confidence. Once he had done this, he found himself in love with her.

For Pitt 1754 was one of the darkest years of his

career. In 1744, after the fall of Carteret, he had become reconciled to the government and for nine years served it patiently in a subordinate post. On Pelham's death he saw his chance for reward. Openly he made a bid for power. There were many, particularly in the City of London, who felt he merited it. But the King disliked him; his friends would not risk royal displeasure to fight for him; he was passed over for high office.

Dispirited, dejected and plagued by gout, he retired to nurse his wounds at the spa of Astrop Wells. In three weeks it had become a 'dungeon': he was nervous, irritable and could not sleep. The rest of that melancholy summer he spent with sympathetic friends or alone in Oxford, gloomily watching the undergraduates enjoy themselves.

In September he had meant to visit his favourite cousin, John. It was only at the last minute that he changed his mind and set course for Wotton. Here at least he could be sure of a warm welcome, although this tired, ill, middle-aged statesman was very different from the brilliant, eloquent young man who had dazzled Stowe and Wotton in the 1730s. Above all, he was touched by Hester's friendship and concern. They walked together one morning in the beautiful park by the side of the lake. When they returned to the house they were secretly engaged.

Once Pitt had made up his mind, he was besotted by his 'matchless Hetty', his future wife. Endowed with a strong sense of his own worth, he would never have considered marrying beneath himself. It was no accident that Hester came from one of the first families in England. He was proud of her dignity and bearing and the fact that, in her own right, she was already a great lady. Furthermore, as an aspiring politician, the union would be a visible seal on his alliance with the Grenvilles.

They had one more week with each other and their

secret before at the beginning of October, Pitt left Wotton. The very next day Hester wrote to him, seemingly lonely and depressed. But in future letters she was to be the calming influence. Pitt even refers to her 'kind absence' when he put forward an impracticable scheme for a lovers' tryst. Denied this, he wallowed in delicious nostalgia. 'Those banks of the Pond you so sweetly remember,' he wrote on 3 October 1754, 'to me are every way delightful; how do I love them for your dear Presence there one morning.' He recounts how in spite of gout and a torrential thunderstorm, he had climbed Lansdown Hill and sheltered under a monument to Sir Bevill Grenville, one of Hester's ancestors. From Bath he roamed miles into the surrounding countryside to find a place where he had once seen her happy.

She, in her turn, told him: 'My Fame, my Pride, my Glory, is centred in you.' But she found it difficult to write of her deepest feelings. 'Affectionate compliments' only, preceded her signature. John Wilkes may have considered Pitt the worst letter-writer in Europe, but his letters were more open than those of his restrained thirty-three-year-old future wife.

Nevertheless, the only flaw in Pitt's happiness was his fear that the Grenvilles would oppose the match. 'What . . . have I to lay at her feet', he wrote despondently to his friend, George Lyttelton, 'but a fortune very far from tempting and a health shatter'd and declin'd.' It was not a prospect to impress the notoriously proud and acquisitive Grenvilles and both Pitt and Hester were uneasy about their forthcoming visit to Stowe. They need not have worried. Hester's family, she discovered delightedly, were only amazed that they could have been so blind for so long. Temple dismissed Pitt's finances with an airy wave of his hand. Even Hester's formidable aunt, Lady Langham, approved 'without a But'. Her favourite brother, James, came to thank her in person for giving him 'the one Man in the whole World' he would have chosen for a brother. Obviously relieved she wrote back to him and Pitt, too, wrote to Earl Temple, larding the pages liberally with words like 'honour' and 'sacrifice'.

They did not serve to blind the meticulous George who took over the negotiations for the marriage settlement from his easy-going brother. At one point Pitt found himself so financially strait-jacketed that he had to protest his need for 'elbow-room' in order to live like a gentleman. On their marriage his wife would bring him £14,000 but Pitt was beginning to doubt if the wedding-day would ever come. 'May I most respectfully implore,' he chafed at Hester's solicitor, 'that small niceties of the Law may be waived.'

But it was not in Hester's calm nature to be hurried. She refused a date before 15 November. When the ceremony eventually did take place it was a day later still, although Pitt had wanted it earlier, before parliament opened. But he could not bring himself to cross his beloved Hester. 'Your own first thought,' he wrote, 'I, for that dear reason . . . wish the most . . .' And then, 'The less Preparation, the less spectacle, the less of everything but of your lovely, tender self, is surely best.' Thus, only a few close friends were present at Hester's house in Argyle Street of which they were both so fond. Afterwards, they left for a necessarily short honeymoon. Parliament had already been sitting for two days. They chose their friend Gilbert West's house at West Wickham. To Hester it was always 'loved Wickham' and Pitt, in gratitude, designed a path in the grounds. The Wests had left it crammed with food but Pitt, eager to impress, brought his own chef with still more. It was unnecessary, for they were quite alone.

Pitt emerged from his short honeymoon with renewed confidence and vigour. When he needed it most, he had found a fresh sense of purpose. From now on and in the terrible times ahead when the dark side of his nature took over, plunging him into the depths of despair, it would be Hester alone who could lead him back to the light. She shielded him, planned for him, shouldered most of the household burdens and guarded his health with almost maternal solicitude. She would never even write to him of her own problems. When all was well, she hung back in self-effacing admiration. When his depression struck, she was there ready to protect and care for him. It took a rare loyalty and courage to be able to do so. As her admirer, Elizabeth Montagu, known as the Queen of the Blue Stockings, remarked: 'Beauty soon grows familiar to the lover, wit may be pernicious and many brilliant qualities troublesome; but a companion of gentle disposition softens cares and lightens sorrows.' So Pitt was to find.

Hester's first domestic duty was a new one – to cut down on expense. Pitt was always spendthrift and always short of money. Luckily, his government office as Paymaster of the Forces merited an official house in Whitehall, but he had already embarked on an expensive project for a house of his own. Number 7, The Circus, Bath, was to be as splendid as an army of 'masons, carpenters, plaisterers, papermen etc.' could make it. It was not in Pitt's nature to do things by halves and in houses and gardens he had a consuming interest. As a bachelor, he had visited all his friends' homes to offer advice. At George Lyttelton's seat at Hagley he had assisted in laying out the park.

Now in the Christmas recess of 1755, he sped happily off to Bath, leaving Hester behind in London with the explanation: 'My presence there is necessary in order to quicken the workmen to fit it for habitation in the Spring.' Reports on the slow progress filtered back to Whitehall. 'I have lived today,' he wrote on 30 December 1754, 'in the Circus . . . Architects, mechanicks, engineers etc. filled the place.' Hester, meanwhile, was already considering the decoration. 'Has it ever occurred to you,' she wrote with typical attention to detail, 'to recommend having the paper match'd to the blue of the half damask that is to compose the Chairs Cushions and the rest of the furniture of your room above stairs . . . different Shades is not to be chosen if it can with the same care be avoided.'

But she could not go to see the house for herself. It was too long a journey and she was already pregnant. Her first child, a daughter, Hester, was born in October 1755. Pitt was delighted with 'the little blue-eyed maid' if a trifle envious of his brother-in-law's wife, Mrs George Grenville, 'that happy mother of males'. However, he hastened to reassure Hester with a joke: 'Poor little Dame Hester is not less dear to me than a son and heir to our no estate could have been.' They may not have owned an estate but at least Pitt had a yearly salary of £4000. Now even that was to go.

Hester's love and support had helped to re-establish Pitt as a formidable parliamentary force. Although still a member of the administration, he was no longer content to be a government yes-man. Throughout the 1755 session he let loose a torrent of criticism, attacking government incompetence in the face of a European war which seemed likely to threaten Britain's trade. He condemned George II's ministers for protecting Hanover with 140,000 troops while only 'two miserable battalions of Irish' could be spared for 'the long injured, long neglected, long forgotten people of America'. Naturally, he had his supporters. The Grenville alliance was still powerful and the City merchants backed Pitt. But in parliament he had few allies and he was intensely disliked by the King. On 20 November 1755, along with George Grenville, he was dismissed.

Financially, if not politically, it was a blow. Politically

he was still buoyed up by the confidence his marriage had given him. Pitt had been left legacies by various patrons and friends, including £10,000 from Sarah, Duchess of Marlborough in recognition of his attempts 'to prevent the ruin of his Country', but he was incorrigibly careless with money. The office of Paymaster was an acknowledged plum with enough lucrative side benefits to amass a fortune, but Pitt had refused to take advantage of them. His brother-in-law, Temple, had to come to the rescue. To give him his due he showed unaccustomed tact in offering Hester, not her husband, £1000 per year. She needed it too, now that they had to move from Whitehall.

Briskly Hester set about the task of finding them a new home. She considered a house in Upper Brook Street at £100 annual rent. It was not expensive but kitchen smells pervaded the rest of the rooms. Could they possibly live, Hester wondered, without roast beef on Sundays? Evidently not. The idea was dropped and they temporarily gave up the search for a London house.

Instead, as a country residence, they decided on Hayes Place near Bromley in Kent. Pitt had fallen in love with the house when his friend, Mrs Montagu, leased it. In the summer of 1756 he bought it and moved Hester in almost at once. Mrs West of nearby West Wickham came over to help them settle. She wrote to Hester a long list of instructions, including the fact that, although fish and pork were readily available at Bromley, for weekend meat she would have to go further afield to the Croydon butcher. Hester was happy in the country. 'London sees nothing of her now and very little of him except on busy Parliament days,' commented Henry Grenville later in the year.

Pitt was especially delighted with the 'humility' of Hayes, by which he meant merely the scope for improvement. The ancient woods, soft valleys and countless little streams were ideal raw material for a keen landscape gardener. Hester, who viewed things differently, was delighted too, but for reasons of economy. She worried still about the cost of the house at Bath but Pitt was adamant about not giving it up. To be fair, he went there often to be treated for gout. At the baths he was a familiar figure, swathed in bandages and limping, with the help of crutches, on his one good leg.

In 1756 at Hayes, Hester gave birth to a long-awaited son. Pitt was beside himself with joy, 'talking nursery'. 'Lady Hester is as well as can be,' he wrote to George Grenville. 'She had a sharp time, but not longer than two hours and a half.' The boy was christened John. 'I think the breed will be a good one,' commented a contemporary drily, 'and can't fail to speak as soon as they are born.'

But almost immediately affairs of state took precedence over family matters. War had broken out with France and was going badly for England. Minorca, the principal Mediterranean base had been lost and the war had spread across the Atlantic to threaten British possessions in North America. The country clamoured for Pitt. He responded with his old arrogance. 'I *know* that I can save England, and that no one else can.'

After one false start when the King dismissed and then was obliged to reinstate him, he was as good as his word. In 1759, the 'annus mirabilis', excitement over Wolfe's victory at Quebec and Hawke's at Quiberon Bay, reached the remotest corners of England. Hester at Hayes knew of the capture of every cannon and mule-train. Pitt dashed off countless notes to her, to be carried by a special messenger on horseback. Almost always she replied excitedly by return. 'My joy upon the news sent me by you, my Dearest Life, was inexpressible,' she wrote after the victory at Louisbourg in 1758. 'I have been obliged to take a whole hour to compose myself in, before I could find the words to tell my Adored Man the infinite delight which I receive from this most glorious and happy event . . . I feel all your joy, my Life, the joy of the dear brothers . . . the joy of the people of England.' She had always believed in his genius and this, above all, made up for the long years of waiting.

In 1758 and 1759, Hester had two more children, Harriet and 'stout William', both born at Hayes. Of the latter, Hester wrote with remarkable foresight, 'I cannot help believing that little William is to become a personage.' Pitt galloped down from London to be with his growing family whenever possible. Now that he had another appointment, he had taken a lease on Number 10, St James's Square, henceforth known as Chatham House. He kept it till 1761 and Hester evidently spent some time there: she had a 'blue dressing-room' which she loved. But for lengthy stays, she seems to have found it rather cramped. 'There is to be a meeting of the Cabinet here this Evening,' she wrote on one occasion to a friend, 'which Always engrosses my Apartment.' From there, when work kept him in London, Pitt would write 'a dispatch to my adored angel . . . infinitely more interesting and important too, than all I could ever address to all the potentates of Europe'. Then he would wait 'with longing impatience . . . for the groom's return with ample details of you and yours. Send me,' he begged, 'a thousand particulars of all those *little-great* things which . . . so far exceed in attraction, all the *great-little* things of the restless world.'

When Hester went to Stowe to see her family, Pitt held the fort. Nursery bulletins reached Hester almost daily. John was recovering from sickness and 'will soon be a ruddy yeoman of Kent'; little Hetty, 'drunk with spring and joy', had tried to chase a butterfly; 'the old gentleman' was 'as well as can be expected' and hoped to go haymaking with the children.

But in fact, Hester's absences made Pitt nervous. Beset

by problems over the conduct of the war, he missed her steadying influence and could find 'delight and consolation' only in her letters. Hester's response was calm and sensible: he must try not to 'weare the mind to pieces by indecision, but to take one's party as appears best, and submit the rest to Providence'. Still, she was distressed that she was not with him 'to sit by your deare side and to try to divert your thoughts from too constant an attention to unpleasing Circumstances'.

Perhaps even at this stage she had begun to sense the troubles that lay ahead. Elsewhere, Pitt was regarded as invincible, all-powerful, the saviour of the Empire. Bonfires were lit to celebrate the victories of the Seven Years' War. In France his name inspired fear and dread. It was a supreme triumph, but for Pitt it spelled disaster. Alternating with bouts of severe depression, he had long experienced phases of manic activity when he was over-confident, overbearing, quarrelsome, arrogant, verging on megalomania. This side of him came to the fore now, brought on perhaps, ironically, by his well-deserved success. Hester, who had to cope with the consequences, especially his quarrels and subsequent solitariness, must have recognized the signs. Pitt's family were also aware of his weakness, although the illness had not taken deep root yet – it was about to do so – and euphemistically called it 'gout in the head'. Knowing that Pitt suffered from gout, they thought the two must be related. Pitt's particular brand of depressive mania was not recognized by medical science at this stage. It was remarkable that in the circumstances, he could remain so long in public life. Partly this was his own doing: as the symptoms worsened, he instinctively withdrew from strangers. He became formal, unknowable and deliberately remote. But Hester also played her part as his bridge to the outside world. With enormous courage and loyalty, she thought and acted for both of them and to a large extent it was due o her that Pitt could conceal the truth.

By 1761 Pitt's colleagues were finding him increasingly difficult to work with. Any kind of criticism he treated as a personal affront. The new King, too, George III, and his favourite, Lord Bute, wished to be rid both of him and of the war. George longed for the day when 'that mad Pitt' was 'treated according to his deserts'.

This was not long in coming. By now the feeling in the country was for peace. Pitt alone urged taking the initiative in a fresh strike against Spain. Out of temper with the people, he could not carry the Cabinet with him either. There was no alternative but for him to resign. In the course of doing so, he made a grave mistake. Refusing a pension for himself, he nevertheless accepted the barony of Chatham for his wife, along with £3000 a year, collected from the sugar duties. Bute was quick to use this against him. The press was filled with scornful jibes at 'Lady Cheat'em'. Most damaging of all was the reaction of the middle class who were in uproar to find that Pitt, the 'Great Commoner', their hero, had after all feet of clay. Defensively, for Pitt's family were by no means enthusiastic either, Hester wrote to Anne, his sister: 'We do not doubt of the share you will take in these gracious marks of his Majesties Royal approbation and goodness.'

Pitt's response to the proposed peace terms was characteristically theatrical. Stricken down by an attack of gout, he had himself carried to the House, swathed in flannel bandages and dressed in black to accentuate his pallor. For over three hours in a feeble voice, he spoke against over-generous peace terms for France. Afterwards, he left London, ostentatiously disposing of his carriage and his town house.

In fact, these economies were for show only. For the next two years, Pitt lived like a prince at Hayes, surrounded by an army of blue and silver-liveried servants, incurring mountainous debts. In 1765 Hayes was sold, but again, through no wish to economize. On the contrary, much to Hester's anxiety, Pitt had found a new toy to lavish money on: he had been left an estate in Somersetshire, Burton Pynsent, by an eccentric supporter. Joyfully, he bore Hester off to Langport to look at it. They found an ungainly, sprawling house, an incongruous mixture of several different periods but with well-proportioned rooms and a justly famous view. Within a few months Pitt had embarked on expensive alterations. A new west wing was built to house his extensive library, mainly history, classics, books on America and the law of nations. For Hester there was a 'bird room' at the end of a long corridor, far away from the noisy children's quarters in the main house. There was already a fine park and well-tended garden but Capability Brown was called in to create a 'natural' landscape. Pitt loathed formality in gardens and planted cypresses and cedars for privacy, sending for them by carriage at vast expense. When the saplings arrived the servants were sent out to plant them as Pitt directed. At the height of his illness he still remembered the exact location of every tree and shrub.

By Christmas 1765, Hester and Pitt had settled in. They found Burton Pynsent 'as comfortable winter-quarters as Hayes . . . the Metropolis is no inviting scene'. Hester was always pleased when Pitt had a new interest to occupy him. 'I am many hours every day in the field,' he told the local doctor, 'and as I live like a farmer abroad, I return home and eat like one . . .' Hester, meanwhile, took over the dairy, to the astonished admiration of her country neighbours. 'She is a woman of business,' one farmer is reported to have remarked. 'What a fine woman to breed out of!' came the reply.

Hester's children were now old enough to join in the family rides and picnics or the long winter evenings when they wrote and performed plays. Even Pitt tried his hand with a lugubrious five-act tragedy. On other occasions they read the classics aloud but Pitt would refuse to read the passages of buffoonery. It was against his dignity to play the fool. That Hester's children were close to her is obvious from their letters, which are spontaneously affectionate and not at all formal. Her daughters, unusually, for the time, were extremely well-educated, having been tutored alongside their brothers. Whether this was Hester's idea or Pitt's, we do not know. From birth, several of the children had delicate constitutions and Hester worried a great deal about their health. In 1773, when fifteen-year-old William went up to Cambridge, his anxious mother wrote, 'I hope Pam [his nurse who accompanied him] will have infused Ideas of buttoning coats, and using particular caution if Cambridge weather resembles ours.' It was lucky that Hester had 'Pam' to rely on, for so much of her time was devoted to Pitt. He had already quarrelled with Anne, his favourite but equally domineering sister. Now it was the turn of Hester's family.

Pitt had been approached several times in his country retreat and asked to rejoin the government. Stubbornly and uncompromisingly, he refused. Meanwhile, once again his vanity threatened to reach megalomaniac proportions. Pale, gaunt and suffering from nerves and insomnia, he brooded feverishly over his enemies, real and imaginary. Among these 'dark, creeping factions', he placed most of his former friends, including Hester's brother, George Grenville. Patiently, she bore with his whims.

Nevertheless, Pitt's popularity among the people was stronger than ever, too strong to be resisted. In 1766 the King gave in to his terms: he was created Earl of Chatham and empowered to form a non-party ministry. With all possible speed Pitt drove to London by coach. 'At such a rate! Lord a mercy!' commented a Burton Pynsent servant who reported passing him on the Marlborough road.

From the start the ministry was a bitter fiasco and for this Chatham himself was almost solely responsible. Even beforehand he had quarrelled angrily with Temple, who was insulted by his patronizing attitude and retired in high dudgeon to Stowe to sneer at 'that great luminary, the Great Commoner'. Hester, who must have suffered greatly from the widespread dislike of her husband, tried to make amends, at least within the family. Acknowledging the disagreement over what she called 'public situations', she nevertheless wrote to her brother, Temple, to suggest a private visit. He refused, curtly. Hester's next letter was sorrowing but proud. Obviously she had made a mistake in believing possible what she so much hoped for, but 'you know my faith, and I hold it fast, that the blessing of Heaven will still be given to upright and virtuous intentions'. Meanwhile, close as she was to her beloved brothers, she loyally stood by Chatham.

He had ignored both her distress and her attempts at peace overtures, wrapped up as he was in his grandiose designs. Indeed, he could not help himself. Now that he had the title he had thought necessary to his dignity, he resolved to govern by dint of his own prestige and with the support of the King. George III naturally welcomed his seeming change of heart. His fellow ministers did not, but Chatham dominated them easily, lecturing them, carping at them, treating them, as one observer said, like 'inferior animals'. For the moment he was secure in the knowledge of royal favour: the only threat came from within himself.

He had four weeks of feverish activity but it was already evident that he had lost touch with reality. When it did come, his collapse was complete. It was to be two years before he could be capable of lucid thought.

In February 1767, Hester had advance warning of his breakdown when he fell ill while journeying to London. For two weeks he lay helpless at an inn in Marlborough and then struggled painfully on. But three 'hot nights in town' laid him low again. This time Hester bore him off to the peace of a friend's house in Hampstead.

There Chatham, in a state of profound melancholy, existed like a hermit in a small top-floor room. He would sit for hours in silence, unaware of any visitors, leaning over a table with his head in his hands. So great was his distress that even Hester was often not allowed to see him. Instead, when he wanted something, he banged with his stick on the floor. A servant would serve his meals to him through a hatch in the wall. From time to time he was possessed by extraordinary fancies. He begged the owner of the house, Charles Dingley, to build on thirty-four extra bedrooms and then raze to the ground the surrounding houses so that they would not spoil his view.

Faced with the fact that bleeding had failed, Hester called in Chatham's doctor, Addington, a distinguished physician who also had some reputation as 'a mad doctor'. His method was to try and bring on Chatham's gout in the hope that when it was cured, the 'gout in the head' would disappear also. 'Two glasses of plain Hock and two glasses of *red port* every day' was the treatment he recommended to Hester, 'over and above the Madeira . . . and the Port which is taken in sago'. Chatham was plied with red meat, kept ready on a spit day and night, and totally deprived of fresh air and exercise. Not surprisingly, there was no improvement and in August 1767, Hester was given power of attorney. The mere mention of business was enough to bring the tears to Chatham's eyes. Nevertheless, he was still in office. The King was reluctant to part with him and clung to every favourable report.

Hester was thus left to deal with much of the day-to-day conduct of affairs. In her own hand, she wrote letters to the cabinet, under the heading, 'My Lord commands'. Chatham's political colleagues wrote back directly to her, but the country as a whole had hardly realized the extent of her husband's collapse. In September 1768, his few remaining supporters in the cabinet sent the Duke of Grafton to gauge the seriousness of Chatham's condition. Hester received him and proved cautious but frank: 'My Lord's Health is very bad . . . (there is) but small prospect of his ever being able to enter much again into business.' Shortly afterwards the King at last allowed his ailing Prime Minister to resign.

For a time all Chatham could think about was the re-purchase of his former house at Hayes. It had become an obsession with him, and Hester, who could deny him nothing, begged the reluctant owner to let it go. It would save her husband; her children's children would pray for their benefactor as long as they lived. And so it was done. The family moved back into their old home. Hester desperately tried to fan the spark of interest her husband had displayed. 'The oak is fallen,' she wrote, striving to interest him, 'the scrubby elm is down and the lawn looks much better as you knew before it would.'

She, who had been so brave for so long, was now at last beginning to falter. She missed the support of her brothers whom loyalty forbade her to approach. When Temple finally wrote to offer comfort, Hester's reply held a plaintive note. Seeing her brother, she wrote, 'would be a balm that would cure her affliction,' namely, 'all the grievous wounds that have been given to every part of my happiness'. In 1769, while she was at her lowest ebb, Chatham at last began to show signs of recovery. For two years he had been sunk in apathy, indifferent to the world outside his small room. Now anger at the drift of affairs in America, where the colonists were being forced into open rebellion, cleared the shadows from his mind and brought back his appetite for life. For once, Hester seized the advantage to bring about *her own* dearest wish: with her brothers Temple and George Grenville, a grand family reunion took place at Stowe. Afterwards, Chatham returned to London in high spirits. For him it marked an important political gain.

The sudden energy he now displayed was formidable, almost like his early days in parliament. One government fell as a result of his ferocious tongue-lashings. But it was too late for Chatham ever to regain power. Parliament listened to his speeches but would not follow him, while the King had resolved never to call upon him again. He could whip up a frenzy of support in the country but he could not lead his party in day-to-day political life. At home again, in the rural quiet of Burton Pynsent, he virtually admitted as much. 'I am now at peace.'

Instead, he turned his attention to 'improving' Burton Pynsent, making plans on a vast scale, with no thought for the cost. He professed to have become interested in farming and built a palatial, pillared farmyard to house the horses and cows. A servant was sent out to buy brood mares and a prime stallion until the experiment became so expensive that a bailiff had to be called in. Next, Chatham returned to his old hobby, landscape gardening, organizing the entire household to plant trees and shrubs, sometimes even by torchlight. On another occasion, in even more extravagant mood, he commissioned Joshua Reynolds to paint a number of his old colleagues for the ballroom.

By 1770 Chatham's creditors were creating a scandal and bankruptcy loomed until Hester intervened. Her marriage settlement had been squandered and the future of her children put in jeopardy, but her one aim in her 'oeconomicals' was to cater to Chatham's whims. Nothing must be allowed to upset or worry him. Alone she dealt with creditors, sold land and arranged mortgages and herself acted as bailiff for the Burton Pynsent estates. 'She is,' commented Coutts the banker admiringly, 'the cleverest *man* of her time in politics and business.'

But it was not enough. 1773 saw the sale of Chatham's house at Bath, while Hester was already making plans to dispose of Hayes. A loan from Coutts gave her a temporary respite and Temple, too, advanced £1000. But almost immediately, James Charles, her youngest son, born in 1761, had to be bailed out of financial difficulties. The news was kept from Chatham, who was again ill and depressed. By April 1777, Hester was desperate. 'I don't know where I am,' she wrote, swallowing her pride, to a relative, 'for it is of the utmost importance to my Lord's Recovery that he shou'd not be acquainted with this circumstance.' If she could be lent £1000, it would be 'more *by half* than the demand . . . but it has distress'd me so thoroughly that I shall not feel at ease without a reserve . . . my Lord being better, may think of a journey, or something that may make an immediate call, which it might be unfortunate not to be able to answer'. It must have been a bitter experience for Hester, who was born a Grenville, to have to beg and borrow without pride from her friends. In the end, it was the Hoods, her cousin's family, who helped her out. They rented Hayes, tried to interest would-be purchasers, and in all, lent Hester over £10,000.

From start to finish, Chatham had been oblivious of the whole catastrophe, for Hester insisted on carrying her burden alone. In any case, his madness was taking over now. He had become obsessed with the idea of disturbances caused by his children, and Hester sadly arranged to keep them away from home. She herself could never escape. 'I cannot ever be sure of a quarter of an hour free from some call or other from my Lord, who cannot sustain without too much emotion, the idea of any friends being here, and he unable to see them, which God knows, he has not the strength to do.'

But it would not last for long. Hester knew that her sixty-nine-year-old husband was dying. 'My poor Lord,' she wrote simply, 'goes on just the contrary of our wishes for him.' Much to her anxiety and against the advice of his doctors, he insisted on speaking one last time in the Lords. His son William was with him as the House stood to hear him in respectful silence, but the speech when it came, was inaudible and confused. Half-insensible from the great effort, Chatham was carried back to Hayes. He died there, on 11 May 1778. Hester, ill with grief, did not attend his state funeral in Westminster Abbey.

Hester was now in her late fifties. In the twenty-three years left to her, she had to contend with many other misfortunes. In 1780 her son, James Charles, was killed at sea, aged only nineteen. Now, within the space of a few years, she also lost her two daughters, Hester and Harriet, both of whom died in childbirth. The second time she seems to have sensed the danger in the last months of Harriet's pregnancy and fretted to join her daughter, although she was clearly too ill to go. Afterwards, she was prostrated. A friend said: 'Hester weeps inconstrain'd and speaks continually of this beloved daughter.'

It was her son William who picked up the pieces. He was the centre of her life now and persuaded her to move to London where he had just joined the House of Commons as an MP. 'My lot will be at the Treasury, as Chancellor of the Exchequer,' he wrote to his mother at the grand old age of twenty-three, 'or in the Home department as Secretary of State.' And indeed, in 1784, she saw him follow his father as Prime Minister.

Hester's other consolation was her orphaned grand-daughter, another Harriet, who came to live on the estate at Burton Pynsent. She was clearly the centre of attention and Hester cooed about her to her friends: 'I wish you cou'd see how pretty the little creature looks and how lively and merry . . . the whole Assembly attended her undressing with the most perfect good Humour.'

The 'little creature' was already a rich heiress, while her grandmother, once more in debt, was forced to borrow money from William. When she died Hester left little but a silver tea urn and her horses and chaise, plus four silver bottle frames, '*bought* by myself'.

Yet she had provided a house for another motherless grand-daughter, Lady Hester Stanhope, daughter of Hester Pitt and Lord Mahon. Spirited and eccentric, this Hester was devoted to her grandmother and wrote her uncle William long bulletins about Lady Chatham's health.

By June 1802, the news from Burton Pynsent was ominous. 'Dear Grandmamma's health,' wrote young Hester, 'having undergone so great a change since I arrived in the winter has been in times the source not only of uneasiness but of melancholy reflection, as when I once part with her, I have little chance of ever seeing her again.'

Nevertheless, Hester Stanhope chose to leave England to travel in Asia. When she returned in spring 1803, her gentle, long-suffering grandmother had already been put to rest, as she had wished, in the Chatham grave at Westminster Abbey. On her grave should have been written, the words she once said to her husband: 'I am not so much mine as I am yours.'

Lady Peel

Imperial India in the 1780s stood on the brink of violent revolution. Even Warren Hastings, Governor of Bengal, was forced, in a very un-British manner to admit that, 'we are faced with a war either actual or impending in every quarter and with every power in Hindustan'. Among Hastings's commanders in the field was a certain Lieutenant-Colonel Floyd, a bluff, gallant cavalry officer who had begun his army career at the tender age of twelve, and shortly afterwards had his horse shot from under him at Emsdorf. Posted to India in 1782, he soon, in spite of the wars, found bachelor life boring. 'I propose marrying,' he wrote to his sister in England, herself a spinster, 'and having a prodigious number of children.'

The first Mrs Floyd seems to have been a nervous, retiring woman. Her husband wrote that, although she had been brought up in India, she disliked and feared her Indian servants. However, she was a devoted wife and mother, insisting on caring for her children herself and writing her husband shyly affectionate catalogues of their doings on army regulation size paper – $2'' \times 6\frac{3}{8}''$, rolled not folded.

By 1795 she already had two children: Henry, destined to be a soldier also, and the quick-witted Miranda. Julia was born in November at the height of one of the stormiest periods of the war. With the birth of her younger sister, Flavia, the family was complete.

By 1798 John Floyd, now a major-general, was longing for home. Two years later he was back and at once started to search for a house; India had served to make his fortune as well as his reputation. The children, meanwhile, were sent to the Reverend Sketchley in Parsons Green until the united family settled happily near Farnborough Hill.

Then tragedy struck. In January 1802 both Flavia and Henry caught scarlet fever. Little Flavia died soon afterwards but her heartbroken mother insisted on nursing Henry through his illness. Henry recovered but Mrs Floyd caught the fever and died. She was still only thirty, and it was her children, among them Julia, aged seven, who had to bear the brunt of this double loss. The two girls had been sent away; one of them was now brought home very ill and along with their father and a few of the maids slowly and painfully recovered. Although physically restored to health, the emotional strains must have been considerable. Julia certainly was never free with her affections until Robert Peel found the way to her heart.

An aunt in Bromley now looked after them but their father remained in close contact, writing them quaintly military-flavoured homilies about their studies. They were to read to improve their minds but 'solid sense – history, poetry, Shakespeare's plays, Pliny's letters'. Novels were to be spurned, 'for ninety-nine times in a hundred they are sad stuff and very poor in thought'. Whatever they read, it evidently did not leave much impression on Julia. She was far from well-educated and in due course her husband was to have to draft her letters.

In 1803, now a lieutenant-general, he was sent to Ireland. In the year of Trafalgar, 1805, he married again. His new wife was very different, a sharp, worldly Irishwoman, 'the comely Lady Denny', described by an acquaintance as a 'gay widow' who yet 'made him an excellent wife'. She was also an excellent step-mother at least with regard to match-making. Miranda was married early and very satisfactorily to an officer in the Coldstream Guards. Now there was only Julia to be settled as befitted the daughter of a newly-created baronet.

To Lady Floyd's delight, the opportunity presented itself right on their Dublin doorstep. She was already friendly with the sister of the rising young statesman who was Ireland's Chief Secretary. Now with Julia she was invited to the Secretary's Lodge by Robert Peel himself. She had every reason to be hopeful. In 1816, at twenty-one, Julia Floyd was an acknowledged beauty, much admired for her oval face and dark-chestnut ringleted hair. That same year in London she had attracted attention from the future Tsar Nicholas and he retained his admiration until his next visit, twenty-eight years later, a fact which even Queen Victoria noticed and commented on somewhat sourly. Small wonder that she captivated one of the rising stars in the political hierarchy.

At twenty-eight, Robert Peel was rather a forbidding figure with red hair, a long face, and, according to Rosebery, 'a certain slyness of eye'. To the rowdy, hard-drinking group on the Tory back-benches he was something of an enigma, being too busy ever to have got married and too fastidious for casual affairs. As a result, his name had never even been linked with a woman's. On the contrary, he had spent the eleven years since leaving Oxford almost totally in masculine company, either at work or in his favourite recreation – shooting. He was ill at ease in drawing-rooms, clumsy and uncomfortable with women. Nevertheless, by 1816, he was beginning to appreciate the gap in his life. His retirement as Chief Secretary in 1818 gave him the time he needed to win round Julia.

He had an indefatigable ally in Lady Floyd who seems to have made strenuous efforts to keep in contact. In 1817 she even volunteered to find some china to add to Peel's dinner service. Eventually, a shipment of Dresden arrived from France and in telling Peel, Lady Floyd seized the opportunity to mention Julia. 'Miss Floyd agrees with me in thinking they are very much in the style of your service . . . Miss Floyd joins me in requesting that you will remember us and . . . believe that we never do or can forget your kindness to us at Dublin.'

By this time the Floyds were back in London at a house they had bought in Mansfield Street. The following year Peel too returned to his tiny, Stanhope Street bachelor house. Lady Floyd immediately prepared to deliver the china, making sure that Peel knew of a visit to be paid them by his sister. Peel duly presented himself also, and from then on his friendship with Julia seems to have prospered. By March 1820, they were secretly engaged.

But from now on the strict conventions surrounding early-nineteenth-century engagements took over. While Julia stayed in London, propriety dictated that Peel should leave town. A residue of reserve made him sound indifferent as he wrote from his self-imposed exile in Bognor that he would 'purposely avoid' 'impassioned declarations' which 'I am . . . satisfied . . . are unnecessary to convince you of the ardour and constancy of my attachment.' His caution is understandable. After all, he had had no chance really to get to know his fiancée before they were separated, and such were the ethics of contemporary engagements that it was open to surmise when he would be able to do so. However, as he became accustomed to writing to her, he gradually lost some of his self-consciousness. He complained quite openly about her own failures to reply to his letters. 'Not one line from my dearest Julia, not even the direction of a letter. The arrival of the post is the only moment of any interest, and when it brings nothing from you, I open what it does bring with great indifference.' 'I for my part,' he added, 'do nothing but write to you and look at the sea, and sometimes pretend to read a book.'

Part of the problem may have been the rumours reaching Julia that the Peel family disapproved of the match. However the rumours started, they were certainly unfounded. The Peel family's fortune and title were very recent and they themselves were only too conscious of their plebeian origins. Far from disapproving, old Sir Robert set up a generous trust fund, and Peel's sister, Elizabeth, declared that the marriage was all she wanted. Peel himself wrote indignantly to reassure Julia: 'My father is, as I knew he would be, made perfectly happy . . . I was sure that he preferred you to any other person whom he had ever seen. He says that nothing shall be wanting on his part to promote the happiness of our union . . . If the iniquity of our enemies had been half so great as their malice, surely they might have invented something more plausible . . .'

However, even with this settled, the engagement was by no means all plain sailing. At this late stage Peel himself seems to have had his doubts. In particular, he worried that Julia might find it difficult to exchange the gay society world in which she moved for the busy world of a hard-working politician. Fortunately, Julia knew how to reassure him. 'You are my world,' she is said to have replied.

Soon afterwards Peel returned to London and the engagement was made official. It was greeted with widespread surprise: Peel had been too reserved to confide in anyone. Among the letters of congratulation was one from a former admirer of Peel's, Lady Shelley. In his reply Peel denied that he ever 'made the boast which is attributed to me that my wife would not be a politician'.

In fact, Julia later admitted as much herself, and in any case it did not matter. That was not her worth to her husband; she had other qualities of equal value.

In April 1820 the new parliament met and began discussion on the Bill of Pains and Penalties. For once Peel's attention was elsewhere. He was almost totally engrossed in Julia and in May 1820 paid £1080 for her engagement present, a string of seventy-eight perfect pearls.

Fortunately for Peel's finances and House of Commons business, the wedding was fixed for the following month. It took place on 8 June 1820 in the drawing-room of the house in Upper Seymour Street which Lady Floyd had occupied after the general's death. Shortly afterwards the Peels left for a country house in Mickleham, Surrey, rented by Peel and deep in the Surrey woods. From there they wrote to Julia's step-mother, Lady Floyd, choosing, symbolically, to share a single sheet of paper. For the first time Julia's feelings show through. 'I believe myself,' she wrote, 'to be the very happiest of human beings. I am thank God united to a thoroughly amiable *man* and one *whom I adore*, *for whom* I would willingly risk existence itself . . .'

They were not words that anyone as contained as Julia would use lightly. Perhaps as she came to know Peel better and penetrated his formidable reserve, she saw mirrored in him her own rather lonely, motherless childhood. At any rate, once he had gained her trust, he held prime position in her life. And he, for his part, had the one element he sorely needed – a stable, secure home in which to shelter from the buffets of political life. More vulnerable than any except a chosen few suspected, he relied on her uncritical support and basked in her admiring love. Julia Peel was never a brilliant hostess – her entertaining was done mostly through a sense of duty. Nor was she party to cabinet secrets like the powerful Lady Palmerston. She was not intelligent enough to take a serious interest in politics. She was not even a personality in her own right like the well-loved Catherine Gladstone. But as long as she was there and the home she had created was there, Peel felt able to continue in politics. He was at heart ambitious, but he was also highly sensitive and with the Peel fortune behind him he did not have to work. There were many occasions when, had he not had Julia as a refuge to escape to, he might have deserted 'that infernal place' at Westminster for ever.

For the moment, however, he was preparing happily to take Julia to Drayton, the newly-acquired seat of the Peel family, set in 600 acres on the Staffordshire-Warwickshire borders. Peel's father had pulled down the 'rude and antique' Elizabethan mansion and in its place had erected a solid three-storey house, architecturally undistinguished but suitable for a rich businessman who was not trying to compete with his county neighbours. Thirty years later, the house was to be pulled down once more: it had become too small for the needs of a Prime Minister.

Here Julia passed the early summer months of 1820, gardening – a new interest that would become a lifelong passion; driving with Robert through the park in his tilbury, and getting to know her blunt, irascible but kindly father-in-law. A journey through Europe completed her honeymoon and immediately afterwards, she and her husband returned to London, where Peel was greeted in December 1820 with the offer of a post from Liverpool. He turned it down as he was to turn down a second offer, pleading 'the habits of retirement . . . and the happiness of my domestic life'. Not till November 1821 did he feel ready to re-enter public life; then he accepted the Home Office, a position he would hold till 1827.

His exacting official duties kept him for long periods in London, while for Julia, childbirth and a host of minor maladies made her crave peace and fresh, country air. Thus was set the pattern of their lives for the next ten years. Peel, for the time being, returned to his bachelor house in Stanhope Street, having first settled Julia comfortably where he could visit her, in a succession of rented houses – Lulworth Castle in Dorset which he picked for its mild climate as well as its rough shooting, or Stone House, Broadstairs, when he felt she needed bracing sea air.

Between 1821 and 1832, Julia had seven children, which naturally restricted her movements and enforced long periods of rest and quiet. But there were some country house visits on which she could have accompanied him and her habitual exclusion provoked an uncharacteristically acid response. 'I do not understand,' she wrote to her husband in 1824, 'how the house at Sudburn which you used to describe as small and uncomfortable in bedroom furniture can accommodate such a very large party as the one now assembled within its adulterous walls.' This was in reply to a letter of Peel's in which he rejoiced she was not asked when the host's mistress was present. 'How will you bear,' she could not resist continuing, 'to think of *one*, compared to *fifteen*. I know it is nothing in the scale.' Peel, who was sensitive enough anyway, was totally defenceless when it came to Julia, the first and only woman who had penetrated his guard. His feelings of surprise and hurt were all too real, despite the clumsy pomposity of his answer. 'I will only remark upon this that I would suffer much rather than write such a sentence to you, at a time when I was absent . . .' He signed himself rather stiffly, 'your attached husband, R.P.'

In fact, despite his absences, his thoughts were never far from Julia. She represented the most important and stable element in his life. 'What wickedness and . . . folly,' he wrote of the poor, neglected Duchess of Wellington, 'to undervalue . . . the affection of a wife.' Every leave-taking was heralded by a 'dull and dreary' feeling of 'melancholy . . . leaving my own Julia and all that is dear to me'. Every letter is full of his dislike of society, of its loose morals, idleness, the boredom it held for him. 'The shooting over,' he wrote from Somerley, 'my thoughts are far away and I am sure I must appear to have little pleasure in society.' Or again after a particularly trying visit: 'If I could love you more, the sight of others, and their odious ways would make me do so.'

She in her turn wrote to him about *her* half of her husband's life, making no attempt even to dabble in politics. Marriage, friends, the children's health, plans for holidays, these were the things that interested her and made him come 'down earlier than usual to the office to get my own Darling's letters'. Occasionally, she worried about making grammatical mistakes in her letters and he had to reassure her: 'Do you think . . . if there were an error . . . it would be discovered by me? . . . If there were fifty errors . . . I should never discover them.'

His letters in time came to be perfectly tailored to hers, full of descriptions of country-house life and food, which he knew would interest her. 'One little story for my love,' he would say and launch into a recital of the latest society gossip. Occasionally, he included political information as well, but almost always with the injunction not to repeat it. Otherwise, like Gladstone at the Board of Trade, he was preoccupied with her little commissions, while she in her turn, worried about the payment of his shooting wagers. Throughout their lives, the letters came and went every day, so that when, in January 1827, after seven years of marriage, Peel received no letter for two days, he was able to say: 'It never happened before.'

Their happy self-sufficiency seemed to shut out the rest of the world, a fact reflected in their unsuccessful search for a country home. In 1827 Peel thought they had found one: a 'marine villa' on a cliff overlooking the Isle of Wight. What appealed most was its absolute privacy, with not even a footpath up from the sea. 'We do not take so much interest in the rest of the world,' Peel remarked, 'as it takes in our proceedings.' 'I stayed awake last night,' he added, 'thinking of the happiness we should enjoy together in a place of this kind with our little ones and not an earwig to molest us.'

But it was not to be: too much of their capital was sunk in their new house in London, a fine mansion, conveniently near Whitehall. With the birth of their first child, who occupied the one guest room, it soon became obvious that Stanhope Street was too cramped. It took over a year to find the alternative they sought – a site in a new terrace to be built in Whitehall Gardens. A lease was bought, architect Robert Smirke engaged and by 1824, the house was taking shape. The frontage of 4, Whitehall Gardens was uniform with its neighbours, but distinguished by a massive bay: at the back this overlooked the Thames. The first floor housed Peel's gallery where he hung his ever-growing picture collection including a Rembrandt bought for fifty-nine guineas. To this were added pictures by Rubens, Jan Steen and Hobbema, as well as contemporary works by David Wilkie and Sir Thomas Lawrence. Lawrence, from whom Peel commissioned fifteen portraits, painted Julia twice, in 1825 and 1827. The first portrait was Peel's favourite but the second was more successful, destined as it was to be a companion to Rubens's *Spanish Hat*. It shows Julia at the height of her beauty, heavily jewelled in a fur-lined cloak and a dramatically-plumed black hat.

Peel's artistic purchases and the vast expense of Whitehall Gardens more than outweighed his fairly handsome official salary. In 1825 his father had to come to his rescue and 1831 saw him borrowing money from his brother. Julia's family did not help: on the contrary, they were a financial embarrassment, as her brother, an indifferent businessman, sank heavily into debt. Lady Floyd continually pestered Peel to indulge in some nepotism, but with Julia's full support, he was able to refuse.

Julia had never been over-fond of her step-mother and now, engrossed in her own family, she resented her constant interference. Self-contained as always, she could be ruthless with outsiders who trespassed on her domestic preserve. 'I have ordered myself to be denied if she calls,' she wrote on one occasion in 1824. 'Last night . . . I succeeded in getting rid of further importunities . . . by asking her for just two hours . . .'

However, the move to Whitehall Gardens necessitated more entertaining as Peel now had to share the task of keeping sweet the party rank and file. It was a duty he viewed with something less than enthusiasm and Julia shared his feelings. 'I will do everything in my power,' one letter read, 'to prevent anyone coming to us soon after my return.'

In 1827 Peel had rented Lady Shelley's Sussex home at Maresfield and was about to visit it, when news came of Canning's death in office. Revealingly, while *The Times* criticized other ministers for gathering like vultures, Peel's first instinct was to retreat into the family circle, protected by the high walls and topiary hedges of Maresfield. But the inevitable summons came and with a leaden heart he answered it, finding 'no compensation whatever in the turmoil of the scenes to which I have been summoned, for the happiness which I left last night. Oh believe me, my own dearest life, that my heart is set upon home and not upon ambition.'

The latter sentiment was only partly true: on another occasion, resuming office, he felt 'like a man restored to life'. Julia's presence served to reconcile this despised and well-hidden ambition with the grinding realities of official life. The hard work, the boredom and trivia, the abuses he saw everywhere, were all bearable when Julia and home offered security and peace.

It was therefore with relief as well as sadness that he learnt in May 1830 of his father's death. Now he had a permanent home where he could settle his family in safety. The funeral took place on 11 May with the reading of the will to follow. Immediately afterwards, Peel wrote to Julia, who had evidently worried that a dispute with his father might have prejudiced their inheritance: 'You may be quite at ease . . . the will is what I always told you I thought it would be . . .'

For the past two years, Peel had been Home Secretary under Wellington. By now the strain of office had taken its toll on him, particularly as he often worked a fifteen-hour day. Too fastidious to cultivate the backwoods squires who were the backbone of the Tory party, he had suffered acutely from their spiteful attacks. He needed rest and quiet – and Drayton, and in November 1830, when the government fell, he went there, announcing that he wished to quit public life altogether. His friends disbelieved him and his brother even contradicted him but for the moment he wrote joyfully to Julia, 'Perhaps I shall awake you with a kiss on Thursday morning if you are very sleepy.'

As a result, Christmas 1830 at Drayton was a particularly carefree one with Peel and Julia poring over plans for a new house. A succession of important political guests had confirmed their belief that this was necessary. Mrs Arbuthnot thought the old house 'frightful' and Croker complained that it could only hold four guests.

Once again they called in Smirke, their London architect, as well as Gilpin, a fashionable landscape gardener. Progress on the house was slow, but it was quicker in the garden, possibly because that was Julia's first love. Nevertheless throughout 1831 and 1832, Peel could not visit London without a list of commissions. Like Gladstone, he would spend a morning buying candlesticks when he could hardly spare time to open his mail. 'My chief pleasure,' he wrote to Julia, 'is to do something connected with Drayton . . .' His main anxiety was 'that people will fret and worry you . . . and not make any allowance for the state of the house . . .'

By December 1835, they were finally in residence, and giving their first dinner party for their Staffordshire neighbours. They had built for themselves a vast florid mansion with all the comforts the nineteenth century could provide – proper heating, plumbing, a library, the most 'magnificent . . . in the Kingdom'. Even Queen Victoria found it the most 'comfortable' house she had been in, though none of the visitors admired its appearance. A massive conglomeration of towers, cupolas, stained glass and mullioned windows, it marked the final eclipse of eighteenth-century taste.

But Peel loved it and was never happier than when out shooting with his dogs or inspecting the farms on his estate. In spring and early summer, when he was forced to be in London, Julia would send up baskets of violets, strawberries and new potatoes. She herself would seldom be coaxed away from Drayton, 'the place of all I love best', though Peel was still doing the rounds of various country houses and would write from Belvoir or Burghley, accounts 'to try to amuse my . . . dearest love . . .'

Julia's last child, Eliza, was born in 1832, and after this her health steadily improved. Gladstone, visiting Drayton in 1836, found her a 'matronly lady who seems to combine the fondness and fragility of youth with a mother's practised character'. Certainly her time was very much occupied by her brood of children: visiting the older boys at Harrow and Eton; making sure they travelled safely home from school – 'The flock is all correct'; arranging games like crook sticks for them to play in the holidays; accompanying them on fishing, boating and riding trips. 'It is so happy for me to have them with me,' she wrote, 'and they are all so very loving and affectionate.' Nevertheless, Peel remained at the heart of her universe, and her one wish for her children was that they should reflect credit on him. Copies of his speeches frequently arrived at Harrow or Eton, along with exhortations 'to cultivate the graces of enunciation and of manners', and then rather less ambitiously, 'Be nice about your hair . . . and hands.'

With Wellington's fall in 1830, Peel's career had reached a turning-point. Willing or not, there were many who saw him as the only saviour of the Tory party. 'Peel,' wrote Greville, 'will be the leader of a party to which all the conservative interest of the country will repair; and it is my firm belief that in a very short time (two or three years or less) he will be Prime Minister . . .' In fact, the summons came in 1834, a year which saw Peel and Julia in Italy where they shopped in Rome and visited the artists' colony. They were at a ball given by an Italian duchess when a message came ordering Peel home. Leaving Rome at 3 a.m. on 26 November, they arrived in Dover late on 8 December. Peel summed up the rigours of the journey in a letter to his brother: 'Julia travelled over Alps, precipices and snow, eight nights out of twelve in the carriage.' The next day, 9 December, Peel went to St James's Palace and found himself the new head of the government.

In fact, it was a government fated to last only a few months, but Peel gave all his energy to it, driving himself on furiously and keeping the separate departments under his overall strict control. In addition, he had to bear the brunt of the political entertaining, which took place when he was alone in London. His father's legacy had left the Peels very rich but they spent to the hilt to maintain a lavish style of life. Guests to dinner at Whitehall Gardens would be received by five powdered footmen, while flunkeys on each landing announced their names, and servants in purple and orange livery served food off silver plate. The Peels were famous for their hospitality. Disraeli, a guest in 1839, mocked his twenty-five fellow trenchermen, 'grubbing in solemn silence'. But the dinner he pronounced 'Sumptuous . . . the second course of dried salmon, olives, caviare, woodcock-pie, foie gras, and every combination of cured herring, etc., was really remarkable.'

Although the onus fell on Peel he had a large staff to help him – fourteen male servants by 1846 – and Julia took nearly all the responsibility for Drayton, paying the bills and sorting out problems with the staff. She did her share of entertaining there too, albeit reluctantly. Peel held annual shooting parties for his political colleagues and in early autumn, Drayton was seldom free from guests. He would write to warn her who was invited, adding anxiously, 'Will you send for fish to Birmingham?' Then the Jerseys would arrive to shoot partridges in the stubble, or Croker, Hardinge and Goulburn, the statesmen Julia knew best. In 1837, before the election, she organized breakfast for one hundred Tamworth voters. But she was still reluctant to accept outside engagements. 'I was civil to all,' she said flatly of a ball in Tamworth, 'and spoke to all I knew.'

In 1837 a bad bout of sciatica left Peel, now forty-nine, lame and disabled with pain. And as always in times of stress, a persistent buzzing in his ears caused Julia concern. However, by 1839, he had recovered sufficiently to squire his daughter Tooti (also Julia) through the London season, sending progress reports to her anxious mother about every suitor and every dance. In the end Julia contracted a great political union with Lord Villiers, son and heir to Lord Jersey. The Jerseys brought their name to the match but Julia Peel brought a large dowry, and as Lady Palmerston shrewdly noted, Lady Jersey was 'triumphant'. In fact, relations with the Palmerstons, always political opponents, were more strained than ever at this point and after a skirmish in the House, Peel wrote with malicious glee to Julia: 'He [Lord Palmerston] meant to have it all his own way, and brought down Lady Palmerston, and a party who were to dine with him afterwards to witness his triumph. You never saw a man look as foolish as he did under the flagellation which I gave him.'

This was a turbulent time for the Commons with heated debates over the Corn Laws, while, outside, riots and unrest spread through the Midlands to the North. Peel, in office again in London, was worried for the safety of his family and sent arms to Drayton, instructing Julia to keep them safe and dry. But not for nothing was Julia a soldier's daughter: her reaction was one of anger and her only worry for him. 'When you come from the station do so as quietly as possible. I shall take care not to say when I expect you.' She had mobilized the household 'quietly and vigorously', even laying in a fresh water supply. 'You will know that I was never guilty of a sentimental or ignoble fear,' she wrote and promised rather bloodthirstily that none of 'the vile mob' attacking 'would have left this place alive'.

As it happened, Peel was in more danger in London. Late in 1843 when he was once again Prime Minister, an attempt was made on his life. It failed but in tragic circumstances because the victim was Drummond, his young secretary. Shock and grief left Peel temporarily depressed, but for Julia, the additional worry for his safety kept her confined to bed. Even Queen Victoria, who in the past had disliked Peel, wrote advising him to be 'cautious, and not expose himself after this fearful warning'.

Her letter was a sign that Peel was now becoming accepted at Windsor after the unpleasantness of his first encounter with Victoria. In 1843, as a mark of favour, the Queen and Prince Albert stayed at Drayton. They were met at Tamworth by Peel on horseback with a group of outriders but, in the circumstances, it was a relaxed, informal visit. The Queen attended dinner in pink satin, ablaze with emeralds, and the next day Julia escorted her round the dairy and the farm. She also walked in the garden, no doubt to admire Julia's roses and the stephanotis blossoms climbing in profusion over Drayton's walls.

But this was a brief happy interval in a time of pain and worry, heightened in 1844 when their daughter Eliza fell gravely ill. Scarlet fever was diagnosed and her frantic parents took the first train to Drayton. Prevented from seeing her in quarantine, they could only watch helpless from their steward's house as she gradually began to recover.

For the duration of the crisis, Peel had virtually relinquished his place in the government. Tired and ill and plagued by gout, he had found the last few weeks a considerable strain. Then in 1845, when a further year of office had taken its toll on him, a bad harvest in England and disease in the Irish potato crop raised the bitterly divisive question of the Corn Laws once more. Peel, who in the time of scarcity favoured reducing import duties, a move highly unpopular with 'the country party' among the Tories, was in the centre of the storm – 'abused', said Prince Albert, 'like the most disgraceful criminal'. Julia, who saw politics only in terms of his feelings, tried her best to offer him her sort of comfort. 'I hope you take good food and nourishment and air and warm clothes.' Such was her anxiety that she incessantly begged to come to London. 'If my presence is any comfort at all I am not only ready but anxious to return to town with you. You have but to say, and I . . . will come up the same morning . . . The last week's anxiety and distress has really been too much for me, as now we are separated I thought only of what was painful.' But he needed Julia at home: 'It is better for you and the children . . . to be in the country,' and besides, 'It cannot be . . . long . . . before we shall be together without such interruptions to peace and happiness as there have been for the last four years.'

Peel did try to resign in December 1845 but when Lord John Russell could not form a government, he was forced to soldier on. Julia heard the news with 'deep regret and disappointment'. This was a trying time for her. Alone at Drayton, she was besieged by anxious relatives and opinionated neighbours. She 'read the papers till indeed *all my courage fails me*'; till she felt 'shrouded in gloomy and painful perplexity'. If she gave Peel security, belief in him was almost an article of faith to her, and when he faltered, her whole world trembled. 'I only honestly ask one thing,' she wrote to him pathetically, 'will the justice, wisdom and uprightness of your conduct be manifest? Will praise or justice be awarded you in place of so much cruel abuse?' She had her answer when the Corn Laws were finally repealed and even one of Peel's detractors wrote, 'No living soul could have done this but Peel.'

Such was Peel's domestic happiness that he was able to face the inevitable backlash from his own party with equanimity. In 1846 he resigned for the last time, writing to his friend, Lord Hardinge, from Drayton: 'Lady Peel and I are here, quite alone, in the loveliest weather, feasting on solitude and repose, and I have every disposition to forgive my enemies for having conferred upon me the blessing of loss of power.' The luxury of time was a new experience for both of them, and Peel was never again prepared to forfeit it. He specifically refused an earldom and the Garter, asking the Queen only that she would not send for him in the years to come.

Most of the next two years the Peels spent at Drayton but August 1849 found them in Scotland in a house rented from Lord Lovat. Perched like an eyrie on a rocky island in the fast-flowing River Beauly, it was accessible only by a narrow wooden bridge. Julia wrote south that she had never seen Peel so happy, although with a strange presentiment he thought it unlikely that he would ever see the Highlands again.

He died on 2 July 1850, still in his early sixties. Five days before, a Commons debate on Palmerston's foreign policy had lasted till daybreak. Peel walked home more than usually tired in the early morning sunlight and it was his wife who suggested an invigorating ride. When his horse stumbled, Peel was first of all thrown clear, but then the animal fell on top of him, causing fatal internal injuries. For days he lay in a state of shock on a mattress in the dining-room, his pain so great the doctors hardly dared touch him. They did apply leeches and mercury against inflammation but, given the state of nineteenth-century medical knowledge, he could not survive. His brothers, sons and two friends were with him when he died some time before midnight. Julia had collapsed and was carried swooning from the room.

Shock and horror at the news united the divided country and a vast crowd gathered silently outside the house. In the Lords the great Duke of Wellington could not speak for weeping; half the members of the Commons came dressed in funereal black. Peel had shunned the idea of burial in Westminster and, also in accordance with his wishes, Julia declined a peerage. But she was greatly touched when the Queen made her a present of Peel's portrait.

It was some time before she could answer the letters of sympathy; she took a month even to write to Peel's close friend, Aberdeen. 'I feel sure you will forgive my writing to you. I can hardly say why I do. But, in truth I am so unhappy . . . he was the light of my life, my brightest joy and pride . . .' She was comforted most by letters from Peel's younger adherents, especially Gladstone's comment: 'He is my leader still, though invisible.' At the end of 1850, Victoria found her still 'crushed in agony', but by now another friend, Sir James Graham, thought it was time she was roused. 'While it pleases God to prolong your life,' he wrote, 'you still have most important duties to perform.' By this he meant Eliza: 'It is most desirable that her home should be happy.'

Julia lived the rest of her days in the house in Whitehall Gardens which had been left to her in her husband's will. Towards the end of her life another great tragedy befell her – her third son, William, died of smallpox in India. His older brother, Frederick, did much to comfort his mother – Julia was not on good terms with her eldest son, Robert – but this second grief was too much for her. On 28 October 1859, after an evening with her daughter, herself newly widowed, she suffered a heart attack in the night. Her maid found her body next morning. It was taken for burial back to Drayton, where she had spent the happiest years of her life.

Lady Palmerston

1839 was a year for parliamentary marriages. In July 1839, in the sleepy, country village of Hawarden, a rising young Tory, William Gladstone, had married the beautiful, aristocratic Catherine Glynne. A month later in London, Benjamin Disraeli, his future political rival, had become the husband of a rich, middle-aged widow. But the country had to wait until December for what was to be the parliamentary match of the year, the wedding of the Prime Minister Lord Melbourne's sister, Lady Cowper, to the then Foreign Secretary, Lord Palmerston.

For such a brilliant social and political occasion it took place with the minimum of fuss. There was not even time for a honeymoon. Instead, immediately after the celebrations, the bridegroom left quietly for his desk in the Foreign Office and the struggle to bring peace to the Middle East. Perhaps this was not so surprising. After all this was no sudden impulse of love-struck youngsters. Emily Cowper and Henry John, Viscount Palmerston, had not only known each other for fifty-odd years; for the last thirty of them, they had probably been lovers.

The future Lady Palmerston had emerged more or less straight from the schoolroom at eighteen to marry Lord Cowper and become a leader of fashionable society. So much was inevitable for the daughter of the formidable Lady Melbourne. But this was an age when society and politics intermingled; when the great ladies of both parties held political court in their drawing-rooms; when it was said that, such was their power, they could postpone a debate in the House if it interfered with a dinner party. And to the daughter of Lady Melbourne all this was a natural part of her education.

Her family connections automatically gave her an inside knowledge of Whig party politics. When her brother, the second Lord Melbourne, became Prime Minister, he took her into his confidence. Her own passion for politics and the Whig party did the rest, so that when she eventually married Palmerston, she was almost as well-informed as he. And now that she had an official position, she became a political force to be reckoned with. People asked her to intercede for them with Palmerston. Her house became a centre of Whig society, and more than that, a barometer of English political life. In her drawing-room decisions were made which affected the future of Europe and more than any other Prime Minister's wife, she was to participate in these. In fact, powerful as Palmerston was when he married her, she probably brought him more than he gave her. It is doubtful whether as a former Tory minister, he would ever have led the Whig party had he not married into one of its most ambitious families. Quite apart from what Emily did for him, it was enough for her to be who she was.

That her family achieved such prominence was almost entirely due to her mother. Her father was a genial provincial baronet until Lord North made him an Irish peer. But aided by a vast fortune and a brilliant, ambitious wife, the new Lord Melbourne soon found himself entertaining the foremost society in London. In order to do so, he bought a fine mansion in Piccadilly which Lady Melbourne, helped by her friend and patron of the arts, Lord Egremont, made one of the most beautiful in

London. Here she made her name as a political hostess giving endless parties and receptions 'where pleasure and political influence went hand in hand'. Her children, meanwhile, were left to the care of an old Jersey nurse. By this time there were six of them but only two were in later life close to Emily – Frederick Lamb, her lifelong correspondent and William, eight years her senior. A portrait by Joshua Reynolds shows Emily as a gentle, serious child. Even her mother called her 'a little thing, all eyes'. By contrast her sister Harriet Lamb was plump, noisy and jolly. For another portrait, this time by Lawrence, they posed together in mob-caps and pink sashes.

They were educated as much as was necessary to make them charming, graceful ornaments to society. The few books they read, if any, were such as might crop up in 'good conversation'. In fact, Emily was largely educated by the conversation of those around her, and fortunately, Melbourne House was always full of those distinguished in literature and politics. During dinner in the splendid dining-room, Emily and Harriet would be brought in and presented, perhaps to Charles James Fox with his alarming red face or the Devonshires, the very heart of the Whig party. Sheridan was a frequent and entertaining visitor. The Prince of Wales came so often that there was much talk about him and Lady Melbourne.

But while Lady Melbourne was always in London, her children were sent regularly to the country. Brocket Park on the River Lea was an unpretentious red-brick mansion, although Lady Melbourne had done her best with a magnificent Adam white and gold interior. Here Emily had a more normal childhood with riding, fishing in the river and walking. Here she could play with her two close friends, Sarah Villiers, later Lady Jersey, and Corisande de Grammont, the future Lady Tankerville. All three from eighteen to eighty were the doyennes of

English society.

There were frequent visits to Lord Egremont at Petworth in Sussex where he held fêtes for six thousand women and children, and to Devonshire House to play with the Cavendish children and the Duchess's niece, Caroline Ponsonby, the future Lady Caroline Lamb. Emily disliked her as a child and felt the same about her as a sister-in-law. And there were always children's parties, especially at the Palmerston home at Sheen. On one such occasion Henry Palmerston, arriving home on holiday from Harrow, just missed a house-party of small Lambs, including of course, Emily.

It was a gay life and it became even gayer as Emily got older. In the early nineteenth century several dance crazes swept through England. Emily's closest friends held special practice parties, when in the privacy of a back drawing-room, they could master the waltz or the quadrille. Called 'morning dances', they began at 3 p.m. with a cold lunch beforehand in either Melbourne or Devonshire House.

Two family tragedies were all that marred this carefree time. In 1803 little Harriet died of consumption. Her doctors had suggested a cure in Europe but her parents did not want to venture abroad. Both Frederick and Emily, drawn closer together by their grief, privately blamed them for this mistake. Then in 1805, Emily's eldest brother Peniston died, leaving William, his mother's favourite, heir to the estate and title. Surprisingly in view of her prolonged absence from the nursery, Lady Melbourne had great influence over all her children. Emily in particular, respected and obeyed her throughout the years of her first marriage.

In 1804 Sir Thomas Lawrence had painted Emily Lamb for the second time. His picture shows a soft-eyed, seventeen-year-old beauty whose face nevertheless is full of character – as Sir Thomas knew only too well, having experienced at first hand her obstinacy. He had painted her in a loose-fitting jacket; she made him substitute a more revealing scarf.

At the age of sixteen Emily had already at least one serious suitor. She rejected William's friend, Lord Kinnaird; possibly her mother had other intentions. Certainly as early as 1801 she had been plying the Duchess of Devonshire for information about the young Earl Cowper who had just appeared in society. 'I defy him not to be lov'd,' gurgled the duchess in a letter from Chatsworth. He was handsomer than anyone else and 'Georgiana is quite, quite regretting him'. Poor Georgiana never had a chance. Lady Melbourne swung into action. By 1805 Lord Cowper was calling regularly on them at Brighton. By May 1805, everything seems to have been arranged for he wrote to Lady Melbourne, 'I shall be extremely happy to come to Brocket on Friday and stay till Monday when I think the whole may be declared. Pray do not mention it before we meet . . . you must not go to D. House tomorrow night or I know very well that your looks will betray you.' The next day he wrote to Emily, a rather shy and awkward letter: 'Pray, is it a dream or not? . . . I shall not . . . be easy till our meeting at Brocket tomorrow . . . The last thing that I remember with certainty is that you promised . . . to carry a bottle of Champagne in your pocket to Mrs . . .'s ball by way of encouragement to me to dance.' And then about their future home at Panshanger, 'Thank you a thousand times for your very pretty plans of bridges: I think they are admirably suited to the character of the place but as the choice of everything here remains with you I will not pretend to have an opinion about the execution of them.'

A few years earlier, to gratify a long-standing personal wish, the Duke of York had exchanged his Whitehall home for Lord Melbourne's. The new Melbourne House, formerly York House and now the Scottish Office, was a magnificent Corinthian-pillared mansion. A graceful staircase led to three great rooms on the first floor. It was here on 20 July 1805 that Emily Lamb was married.

She wrote dutifully to her mother while on honeymoon, 'It is owing to you, dearest Mama, that I can thus sign my name inside this pledge of happiness, "Emily Cowper".' Whatever had made her happy, it was certainly not Peter Leopold, 5th Earl Cowper. At twenty-seven he suffered from rheumatism, sat in the Lords and was considered dull. Even Lord Broughton who liked him, admitted, 'He has a slow pronunciation, slow gait and pace.' But if not clever he was reliable and rich and as a Whig, acceptable to Emily's circle. Panshanger, his rambling, grey-stone country seat, was comfortably close to Brocket. At any rate as a married woman, Emily could go where she wanted in society. Her movements would certainly never be questioned by her diffident, slow-witted husband.

So the beginning of the London season saw Emily comfortably settled off Hanover Square. Lord Cowper owned a splendid house in George Street, inherited from a rich ancestor. The south-west corner of the square was taken up by an enormous, rambling mansion, the London home of Lord and Lady Palmerston whose young son Harry was living with them. The two young people already probably knew each other. Society was then so small as to make it unavoidable. And for those who thought the old order might be crumbling, there was always Almack's to reinforce their sense of privilege. For this, the holiest of social holies, entry was by invitation only, while the rules were enforced by seven formidable lady patrons, drawn from the highest ranks of English society. It was them Disraeli mocked in his novel *Sybil*, because they 'think they can govern the world by what they call their social influences'. At any rate their social influences were strong enough for them to turn away the Duke of Wellington himself for being improperly dressed, while of three hundred Guards Officers seeking entry, only six were considered socially acceptable.

In 1810 Emily Cowper was a patroness along with the notorious, bewitching Lady Jersey, while one of the most popular figures at the weekly balls and gambling sessions was the handsome, charming, dandified Henry Palmerston whose nickname, 'Cupid', echoed his reputation and yet who at twenty-five was the youngest Secretary of War the country had ever seen, taking his first steps in politics as Emily took hers as a political hostess. For it was not just society that interested Emily. Politics were the stuff of her being. Linked to her inside knowledge she displayed a cool, quick judgement which led both her brothers increasingly to draw her into their confidence. Melbourne, now in parliament, regularly consulted her and Frederick, a diplomat, depended on her letters for information. Neither of them underestimated her ear for the latest political gossip. 'It's not measures or principles so much as pique and personal likings and dislikings which influence people . . .' Emily maintained.

Her political influence at this point was not nearly as great as it would be but nevertheless as Lady Cowper she entertained some of the most powerful men in Europe. Some years later Charles Greville was a guest at Panshanger and wrote an amused letter to his brother, describing his stay. 'I have been at Panshanger for the last week shooting . . . We have had the whole Conference there. Fordwich asked Auguste (his servant) one morning who was gone. "Ah, my lord, les ministres d'Autriche, de Prusse, de Hollande et de Russe viennent de partir." '

Much of this came about through her growing intimacy with the Secretary of War. But we do not know to what extent Emily was responsible for the change in Palmerston's fortunes – how from being a High Tory minister, he became the Foreign Secretary of the Whigs. His quarrel with Wellington obviously had a great deal to do with it. In 1828 he left the War Office after eighteen years of service. In 1830, on George IV's death, the country had a general election. The Whigs won many seats and it looked doubtful if Wellington could survive. In 1830, aged forty-six, Palmerston became Whig Foreign Secretary. With considerable aplomb he commented, 'We shall drink the cause of Liberalism all over the world.' As Foreign Secretary he became chief to Emily's brother, Frederick. Greville's comment was, 'The Chief is devoted to the sister and the sister to the brother.'

There seems no doubt that Emily had long been Palmerston's mistress. Certainly, the current moral climate and the reputation of both the Foreign Secretary and the lady patronesses do nothing to deny it. In London it was an open secret and in some foreign embassies it became the practice to lure Palmerston to parties by inviting Lady Cowper. *The Times*'s nickname for Palmerston, 'Lord Cupid', was not prompted solely by his penchant for over-youthful, ultra-fashionable clothes.

Indeed he was probably the lover of not one but three patronesses including the 'divine' Lady Jersey of the black hair and perfect skin, still at nearly fifty the most famous society beauty of her day. Luckily her amiable husband refused to fight duels on the premise that he would have to challenge every man in town. Rumours also circulated about Palmerston and Countess Lieven, long-nosed but formidably intelligent and a close friend of Lady Cowper. She created a furore by dancing the waltz with Palmerston in the days when it was still considered brazen to clasp your partner round the waist.

Lady Cowper too, was not famous for her fidelity.

The diarist Creevey called her one of 'the most notorious and profligate women in London'. Palmerston may well have fathered some of her children but so probably did Pozzo di Borgo, an exiled friend of Napoleon's. But these affairs were conducted according to a tacit code in society. What made Emily despise and despair of Caroline Lamb was that the latter dared to do openly what Emily and her mother did in secret. William's marriage to Caroline Ponsonby had been acclaimed as a great Whig union but soon degenerated into a farce and a scandal. Caroline was by nature emotionally unbalanced and unstable but she was not helped by her husband, who regarded her with a mixture of affection and indifference, nor by her ambitious mother-in-law, who used her as a political tool, nor even by her sister-in-law, Emily, who had always disliked her. Emily professed herself shocked by Caroline's association with a lowly Scottish doctor and was genuinely alarmed by the scandal of her affair with Byron. In 1816 when Caroline published her libellous book, *Glenarvon*, she was ostracized by almost the whole of fashionable London. Emily's irritation grew along with concern for William's political future, so that after Lady Melbourne's death in 1818, she concentrated all her energies on bringing about a separation, reporting to Frederick by letter on results. 'Brother Wm is much better in health . . . But he is in a fidget at his affair not being settled . . . He wants energy so much and somebody at his back to push him on . . .' In fact, it was not until 1825 that William could be persuaded into a separation: even then, he felt responsible for his wife and continued to visit her at Brocket. Caroline's death from dropsy in 1828 eventually solved the problem. She was still only in her early forties, but her nerves were shattered and in her last few weeks she had suffered great pain. Emily, however, was pitiless. 'Far be it from me to rejoice at anybody's death,' she commented baldly, 'but I

Lady Chatham as Lady Hester Grenville
in 1750, by T. Hudson

Lady Palmerston
aged about 53, by John Lucas

ady Peel, one of two portraits
y Sir Thomas Lawrence

Lady John Russell with her eldest son, John,
by R. Thorburn

cannot help acknowledging the peace of mind I have acquired by this event, and all the anxiety from which it has relieved me.'

Emily's letters to Frederick, besides being a chronicle of political life, often mention her devotion to Panshanger. She lists in great detail her improvements to the gallery and terraces and adds impulsively, 'I cannot bear to go to London, for I love this place . . . The farmers are many of them paying up, which . . . may perhaps enable us to go on with our building this year.' On the other hand, her devotion to her husband was less conspicuous. She could only manage a stiff little note to her brother, commending 'Lord Cowper's kindness and good nature to me, which is so very great that I really do not know how sufficiently to show my gratitude for it'. However, as the years passed Lord Cowper's name was more frequently mentioned and almost always in connection with his health. He suffered from gout now as well as rheumatism and Emily was preoccupied with a cure for him. She tried lettuce pills, bark, calomel, anything but the dreaded bleeding. 'Damn the doctors, say I.' But it was all to no avail; by 1837 his health was failing. The end came on 21 June and Emily noted sadly: 'At a quarter to nine at night was the last breath of the best of friends and the kindest of husbands. The most benevolent and the kindest of men. The most strictly just and the most considerate of the feelings of others. All his good qualities would fill a page, and his faults were almost none; at least I never knew a mortal in whom was less to blame or more to love and admire and respect.'

In fact she was probably more bewildered than grief-stricken. She had lost her way of life of thirty years. Her son took over at Panshanger and she in future spent much time at Brocket, confiding to her diary, 'How difficult it is to know where to go and how best to live.' Her brothers were anxious about her loneliness and even the Queen tried to reassure Melbourne, saying that at fifty-two Lady Cowper was better-looking than many younger women. Melbourne proudly agreed: 'She was always like a pale rose.' And so she was, with her dark, vital looks and delicate skin.

It was not till August or September 1839 that she made up her mind to marry Palmerston. He had been pressing her for months but she hesitated a long time before finally accepting him. He was now fifty-five but with the habits and pleasures of a much younger man. Only that year there had been an unfortunate incident with one of the Queen's ladies-in-waiting at Windsor. Happily Melbourne intervened and the Queen did not oppose the match. Her reaction (in a letter to Prince Albert) was much the same as the rest of society's: 'They are both of them above fifty, and I think that they are quite right so to act, because Palmerston since the death of his sisters, is quite alone in the world and Lady C. is a very clever woman and *much* attached to him . . . Still, I feel sure it will make you smile.'

But Emily's family were less enthusiastic. Frederick alone advised her to go ahead and do as she liked. Melbourne admired Palmerston as Foreign Secretary but did not want him as a brother-in-law and in any case was worried about Palmerston's financial circumstances. He was said to be deeply in debt and even with Broadlands, his country seat, his £12,000 annual income was much lower than Emily had a right to expect. Other members of the family pointed out that he was only an *Irish* Viscount and worried that, by marrying her ex-lover, Emily would attract even more scandal. Above all, Emily's children were against it. Even Lady Granville who had no love for her admitted, 'She has courage to face her angry children.'

But face them she did although she seems to have begun her new life with misgivings. On 15 December

1839, the day before the wedding, she stayed miserably in her room and wrote in her diary, 'Was alone all day and packing; felt low at former recollections and reading old letters.' Luckily 16 December dawned sunny and fair: 'A beautiful day, which I accept as a good omen, and I trust the event of the day will contribute to our mutual happiness.'

Lord Palmerston was now more powerful than he ever had been and had held office on and off for thirty years. By marrying him, Emily gained an official position and also in a sense a new career. She knew that with her experience she could do much for Palmerston besides softening the edge of his asperity. Politically, they were in complete accord. Although traditionally Whigs the Lambs had conservative views on many issues and in the 1830 struggle over the Reform Bill, Melbourne and Palmerston adopted the same attitude, accepting the bill as inevitable but disliking it all the same. Emily went even further. According to Greville, she was 'a furious anti-Reformer'.

At any rate the way was clear for Emily to fling herself wholeheartedly once again into the political arena at an age when most of her contemporaries were content to become armchair spectators. Her first task was to accustom herself to Palmerston's mode of working, for he had always kept curious and very taxing working hours. He would come in from the House, sometimes in the early hours of the morning, and go straight to work at his specially-designed desk, standing not sitting so that he would not fall asleep inadvertently. The sceptics murmured that he treated work and pleasure with the same zeal and single-mindedness.

Palmerston's industry may have been admirable but his abrupt manner was a drawback for him. Emily immediately saw that it would be to his advantage to broaden his social circle, to keep his doors open not only to his friends and political supporters but also to the waverers, the non-political, even to his detractors. Accordingly over Christmas at Broadlands she gave her first house-party for him, a momentous gathering that laid the foundations for a foreign alliance. Shortly afterwards Palmerston moved from the house in Stanhope Street which he had occupied for the past 33 years to a much larger house in Carlton Gardens overlooking the Mall. Emily was delighted at the size and grandeur of the reception rooms and by March 1840 felt settled enough to write: 'We have been giving some dinner and evening parties which have had a very good political effect, have helped the party, and have pleased many individuals belonging to it.'

She was to help the party even more directly in the 1841 election when she went down to Tiverton to appear beside her husband. But it was to no avail: there were unpleasant interruptions from Chartist hecklers and soon after came the news that Melbourne's government had lost to the Tories. Surprisingly, the news did not meet with despondency in the Palmerston household. On the contrary, a cheerful dinner party was convened to discuss the new government appointments and the next day Emily wrote briskly to Palmerston: 'The fact is our party in government and in the country were growing supine and tired, but I think this change will now alter the whole character of the party and that we shall before long prove stronger than before.' Their own future was much more uncertain. Palmerston owned land in Hampshire and Ireland but he owed much of his security to his income from office. Nevertheless, he now retired to Broadlands to see to the running of the estate.

Broadlands stood in a green and peaceful corner of Hampshire in a fine park with the River Test flowing through the grounds. Part of it was Elizabethan with some exceptionally beautiful oak panelling but an eighteenth-century front had been added with huge porticoes. Palmerston spent his time checking the estate accounts, hunting and walking in the park with Lady Palmerston where they both planted many trees. Where Gladstone felled trees for relaxation, Palmerston liked to plant them and watch them grow. Occasionally he would ride with a groom to his racehorse stables twelve miles away, galloping full tilt all the way, chatting to the trainer, then galloping back. 'Such capital exercise', he would say. In the evening he played his favourite game of billiards; he especially enjoyed it when his wife came to watch him win. Together, he and Emily went to visit his estate in Ireland, driving to see his slate quarries through a heavy snowstorm.

But all this was not enough to occupy the former Foreign Secretary and visitors to Broadlands found him increasingly frustrated and irritable. In January 1842 even the new, young Lady Cowper commented on it: 'Lord Palmerston is bitter as usual, and evidently cannot get reconciled to not being longer Secretary, though he don't appear at all bored from having a great deal to do, but he abuses everything and everybody connected with the Tories . . .'

Fortunately for Emily's peace of mind, he was shortly to discover a new interest which had its beginnings in the 1844 government bill to limit the working hours in factories. Lord Ashley, later Lord Shaftesbury, Lady Palmerston's son-in-law and a tireless champion of working-class interests, criticized the bill for not going far enough and persuaded Palmerston to support him. Lady Palmerston, too, lent her support, though probably less from philanthropic conviction than from loyalty to Ashley because he was married to her daughter, Minnie. At any rate Palmerston and his wife received the factory delegates into their house where a spectator was treated to the improbable sight of Lord Palmerston, helped by a footman, learning the niceties of cotton spinning. As it happened, Ashley's motion failed but it was largely due to his influence that Palmerston found himself increasingly cast in the unlikely role of champion of the working man. Indeed, by 1848, 'the year of revolution', the Radicals themselves had begun to look to him as a leader.

Lady Palmerston, as always, supported him loyally, though characteristically wishing that life with Ashley need not be quite so uncomfortable. Although fearlessly outspoken in her defence of Palmerston – so that after an especially provocative speech, which she made when presented with a portrait of her husband, he had to appeal for silence from the press – she was never likely to forget where her true interests lay. Her diary for 5 April 1848, five days before the mass Chartist meeting, carried the doom-laden prophecy: 'Revolution.' On the day of the meeting itself, she revelled in the excitement and against Palmerston's express orders, insisted on witnessing events, but in the end was unutterably relieved that the mass rally had failed. 'What a wonderful result,' she wrote. 'Can it be really all over? . . .'

Obviously Palmerston's incongruous flirtation with the Radicals could not last but his five years in opposition had brought him national recognition and prestige. He was not so popular within his own party. In June 1846, in order to appoint Palmerston as Foreign Secretary, Lord John Russell had to over-ride many of his Whig colleagues and, indeed, even the Queen herself. It was a significant omen for what was to be a stormy ministry.

The great Whig dynasties had never truly accepted Palmerston. He was, after all, not one of them. He had emerged from nowhere politically, and made his own way through intelligence and determination. They disliked his cockiness and air of jaunty bonhomie. Mistrusted as he was within his own adopted party, he came to rely more on Emily. Her support and sympathy calmed him, her guidance eased his passage with his fellow Whigs. His relations with the Queen were altogether more difficult although there was no visible reason why they should have been. Melbourne had been Victoria's beloved mentor and friend while Lady Palmerston was one of her favourite ladies-in-waiting. But the young Queen, buttressed by her marriage to Albert, resented Palmerston's overbearing manner and the way in which he treated the Foreign Office as his private preserve. As Queen she was a personal friend of most of the monarchs in Europe, but continually found these friendships eroded by despatches sent without her prior knowledge. If she did see a despatch which she wanted altered, Palmerston would often high-handedly cancel it altogether. In 1848, after just such a case, the Queen complained bitterly to Lord John Russell: 'No remonstrance has any effect with Lord Palmerston.'

Lady Palmerston with her customary shrewdness saw the danger and in fact did try gently to remonstrate with her husband. 'I am sure the Queen is very angry with you!!' she warned him. 'I am afraid you contradict her notions too boldly . . . I am sure it would be better if you *said* less to her – even if you *act* as you think best . . . I should treat what She says more lightly and courteously, and not enter into argument with her, but lead her on gently, by letting her believe you have both the same opinions in fact and the same wishes, but take sometimes different ways of carrying them out.' Palmerston did eventually heed her advice though not in time to avoid a crisis. In the meantime to Albert and Victoria he was still 'the immoral one' and relations with Windsor steadily deteriorated.

But if Palmerston had his problems politically, the last ten years had been a time of great suffering for Emily as she was forced to watch the gradual decline of her brilliant brother, Melbourne, into a shuffling, shambling old man. As early as October 1842, her other brother, Frederick, had noted the change in him, on his return from Italy. He found Melbourne depressed and tearful, his mind constantly straying back to his days of glory when he was both friend and counsellor to the Queen. His eyes would fill at the mere mention of her name. While he seldom ventured far from Brocket, he had lost all interest in its management and the estate incomes were slowly dwindling.

Frederick hastened to warn Emily who seems to have been unaware of the danger, but even then neither of them realized quite how ill Melbourne was. The blow when it came was all the more shocking for being so totally unexpected. Lady Palmerston, on the point of boarding her travelling carriage to Tiverton, her husband's constituency, was summoned instead to Brocket. An express letter from Frederick confirmed her worst fears: 'Melbourne has a slight paralytic attack. Thomas the Hatfield apothecary is with him . . . Perhaps you will come but I shall write by tonight's post.' Upon arrival she found 'the alarm and reality all too dreadful', but already Melbourne was rallying; he was to linger on for six painful years yet.

Lady Palmerston's anguish was compounded by what she felt was the need to keep Melbourne's illness secret. She worried that the news, if it were to reach the public, might gravely damage the Whigs. But in 1843 Melbourne had recovered sufficiently, in any case, to contemplate a return to the Lords. The Palmerstons were against it on both political and personal grounds and even Queen Victoria worried about the possible strain. Whatever ill-feeling she may have harboured for Palmerston, she forgot it in her concern for Melbourne's health. A stream of anxious enquiries flowed into Brocket from Windsor and Prince Albert's secretary was despatched to gain news at first hand.

They need not have worried. Melbourne's decline was very gradual. For some years he continued to speak in the House, write letters and visit his friends. Then, little by little, as his faculties failed him he began to spend more and more time within the protective walls of Brocket. He died there eventually on an autumn evening in 1848. After the pain of his last few hours, his sister felt comforted in her bedside vigil to see 'his beautiful countenance, so calm, contented and resigned'. Emily rose from the death-bed of one brother to go to the sick-bed of the other. In the next room at Brocket, Frederick lay desperately ill, tended by his new, young wife. It was an illness from which he was never fully to recover.

It was fortunate for Emily, at any rate, that a crisis in her husband's career now claimed her interest and attention. Her spirits rose as she prepared to meet the challenge. The crisis, foreseeably, concerned Palmerston's rift with Queen Victoria. In spite of Emily's admonitions, their relations had steadily worsened and it seemed only a question of time until matters came to a head. They did so in December 1851 when, among other things, Palmerston accepted an address from some Radicals criticizing the Austrian Emperor. The Queen's reaction was swift: she had had enough of these 'difficulties' and wished to transfer the office of foreign secretary into other, more amenable hands. Palmerston had to go, '*exceedingly* angry', according to a friend '. . . at the manner of putting him out. He didn't go to Windsor to deliver up the seals but sent them by a messenger.' The 'messenger' was Lord John Russell. The Queen and Prince Albert had already waited over an hour for their audience with Palmerston when the Prime Minister intervened and himself delivered up the Foreign Secretary's seals. In fact, Palmerston later apologized and this marked the nadir of his relationship with Queen Victoria as well as the effective end of his phase of flirtation with the Radicals. He had strayed as far from the path of orthodoxy as he dared.

Lady Palmerston's immediate reaction was a mild one. She wrote in her diary that she and Palmerston were thankful to be alone in their carriage going to Broadlands in order to discuss the 'disagreeable' letter just received. However, her comments in other quarters were less innocuous. This was a great personal blow to her. The night of 18 December had been one of despairing sleeplessness. Now she channelled all her frustrations into a vigorous defence of Palmerston, whom she considered the victim of an unscrupulous conspiracy, thus prompting the wry observation: 'Lady Palmerston is taking it to heart *far more than she ought.*' Her letter to Lord John Russell was such that he even contemplated not answering it, but it was to her ailing brother, Frederick, that she poured out her indignant heart.

'John has behaved shamefully ill to Palmerston . . . throwing over a colleague and a friend without the slightest reason to give for it. No doubt the Queen and Prince wanted to get Palmerston out and Granville in because he would let Albert manage the Foreign Office which is what he had always wanted . . . I am still vexed and provoked . . . but I am taking it much more calmly. It is so lucky for an effervescing woman to have such a calm and placid husband which no event can irritate or make him lose his temper.' Calmer she may have been at this juncture but all the same the diarist, Greville, retreated at the prospect of 'a fresh correspondence with Lady Palmerston about *The Times* attacking her husband'.

But in 1852, the resignation of Lord John Russell and subsequent election called by Lord Derby gave her a chance to enjoy a kind of revenge. 'I should say,' she wrote gleefully to Palmerston as he campaigned, 'the speeches and addresses and general tone must have opened Lord John's eyes to his true situation. Nobody praises him or puts his name forward if they can help it – unless it be to abuse him . . .' Emily's political ambitions by this stage left no room for magnanimity, even to a former friend.

Her anxiety for Palmerston to be recalled from the wilderness was noted even at Windsor but for once it was Palmerston himself who seemed to be putting obstacles in the way. He was naturally anxious to join the coalition ministry of Whigs and Peelites formed under the Peelite leader, Lord Aberdeen, but this time it was the Home Office, not the Foreign Office, that he coveted. Promptly, Emily sat down to write to Lord Lansdowne, elder statesman of the Whigs, adding the cautious rider, 'Never let him know I have written this.' The tone of her letter was one of utter candour. She was, she admitted, voicing her 'innermost thoughts, written to you as an old friend'. The theme of 'friendship' was to be a recurring one. Emily was a consummate letter-writer. 'I thought,' she began briskly, 'you seemed very anxious yesterday that Palmerston should join this Government – I am very anxious too as I think it would unite him again with all his own Friends. Now I think that if you could speak to Palm. again and urge him strongly to reconsider his determination that he might perhaps be induced to do so . . . If it is now too late and this letter is useless I trust you will burn it and mention it to no living soul – but if you are willing to try your influence with Palmerston and that it is yet time to do so – pray come here any time either to him or to me –' The last paragraph was a masterpiece of political timing as well as feminine subtlety:

'If besides your opinion and advice which he so much regards you could be empowered to offer the Home Office I think this might tempt him – as it is the place he would always have preferred as he believes it is the

Department in which he could do most good.' A few weeks later Emily was rather grandly informing a friend, 'after many negotiations and many refusals from Palmerston he has at last been prevailed upon by Lord Lansdowne to form part of the new Government'. Needless to say, the post in question was the Home Office. The combination of Palmerston's talent and Emily's influence was irresistible.

The new Home Secretary had aged a great deal and was suffering from gout. Queen Victoria, seeing him walking with two sticks, found him 'terribly altered . . . all his friends think him breaking'. But in fact the prospect of a new term in office rejuvenated Palmerston without in any way endangering a newly-acquired geniality. Even the Queen was charmed by this perceptible mellowing in his temperament and was prevailed upon to invite him to Balmoral. 'Lord Pumicestone' at last gave way to 'Good Old Pam'. Emily was left behind at Broadlands, suddenly 'shorn of its beams by your departure'. Perhaps even more than Palmerston, she had needed the hustle and bustle of office, the continual political excitement which alone served as an antidote to her personal sorrows.

Another blow was in the offing. Her last and dearest brother Frederick was fatally ill at Brocket. On 14 January 1853 Lady Palmerston was sent for. When she left the house she knew it was the end. 'I have lost the best friend I ever had.' Frederick died on 29 January 1853, leaving a widow, 'poor Adine . . . who will not leave his room nor his bed, nor take off her clothes, nor take any nourishment at all' and leaving Emily sole survivor of the once dazzling Lamb family. She inherited not only Brocket, Melbourne and the estates in Lincolnshire and Nottinghamshire but also what was left of her grandfather, Matthew Lamb's enormous wealth. It would end the problem of Palmerston's ever-fluctuating finances but it was scant consolation in her loneliness.

She could of course derive some comfort from her Cowper children but she had never been especially maternal. Her eldest son, Lord Fordwich, bored her and her favourite daughter Frances, Lady Jocelyn, had griefs enough of her own. After six of her children had died in the nursery, her husband contracted cholera while serving in the militia in the Tower. He died in the back drawing-room of the latest Palmerston home in Piccadilly, having stopped off on his way home to his wife at Kew.

Once again politics were Emily's salvation. In January 1855, Aberdeen resigned as Prime Minister after a motion was carried in the House to investigate the conduct of the Crimean War. Both Derby and Lord John Russell tried unsuccessfully to form a government. Finally, the Queen turned to Palmerston. Lady Palmerston's terse entry in her diary belied her tremendous and proud gratification.

4 February 1855: 'Palmerston commissioned to form a Government by a letter from the Queen at six o'clock.' Now, with her family worries at last behind her, she could come into her own as a political hostess.

In 1854 Palmerston had sold the house in Carlton Gardens and bought Cambridge House, the Duke of Cambridge's former home in Piccadilly, now the Naval and Military Club. It was a fairly small house but dignified, with a carriage drive up to the front door and a fine view over Green Park. It was here that Lady Palmerston held her famous Saturday evening parties, Downing Street being kept almost entirely for office purposes.

In his novel, *Sybil*, Disraeli had summed up the rules for a political hostess:

'Ask them [the MPs] to a ball, and they will give you their votes; invite them to a dinner, and if necessary they will rescind them; but cultivate them, remember their wives at assemblies, and call their daughters by their right names, and they will not only change their principles or desert the party for you, but subscribe their fortunes, if necessary, and lay down their lives in your service.' Disraeli of course, had meant it satirically but for Lady Palmerston it was a policy that worked astonishingly well. Political, social and literary London jostled each other for invitations to her assemblies. Whigs, Radicals and Tories mingled happily there with ambassadors and newspaper editors while Emily, with her deep, drawling voice and her peculiar blend of steely determination and gentle charm soothed the wary, wooed the doubtful and rebuked those who had temporarily deserted the fold. She would seek out especially the young men, hoping to influence them into the Palmerston mould. Like the other political women of her day Emily did not participate openly in politics. She did not sit on committees or make impassioned speeches at the hustings; but work she did, and with notable success for both Palmerston and the Whig party.

On several occasions when Palmerston found himself particularly in need of support, Lady Palmerston came to the rescue with, 'Stay! we will have a party.' She would write the invitation cards herself although her daughters were called in to address them while she oversaw preparations in the gracious, candlelit reception rooms upstairs, hung with yellow silk and filled with Emily's beloved Empire furniture.

On the night of the party, the carriages of the guests would fill Piccadilly, while inside an ever-increasing throng waited to mount the stairs, past the official portrait of Palmerston with his despatch boxes. At the head of the stairs, Palmerston and Emily would be waiting, the latter resplendent in diamonds and crinoline, although as one wit remarked, not even the Garter could make Palmerston look aristocratic.

In a political crisis, the room would be humming with suppressed excitement. In 1859 Cobden came and was scrutinized by fashionable ladies through their quizzing-glasses. At other times the guest list included foreign royalty and revolutionaries, while London society rubbed shoulders with Polish and Italian refugees. Queen Victoria objected strenuously to the presence of radical journalists, some of whom were markedly anti-royalist. Palmerston's reply reiterated a statement he had published in *The Globe* a few years previously: Lady Palmerston wished to provide a forum for distinguished people of widely different views. Certainly her invitations were sent out regardless of political animosity. A French diplomat marvelled at it in conversation with Disraeli. 'What a wonderful system of society you have in England! I have not been on speaking terms with Lord Palmerston for three weeks, and yet here I am; but you see I am paying a visit to Lady Palmerston.' It was just the sort of social camouflage that Palmerston found politically invaluable.

Meanwhile Lady Palmerston's influence with her husband thrust her increasingly into the role of mediator. More and more people came to approach him through her. It was one of the things Hayward remarked on in his obituary of her published in *The Times*. 'You must write that down,' she would say, 'and I will show it to Lord Palmerston.' 'The bell was rung, the servant was sent with a scrap of paper or a simple message, and the summons was immediately obeyed. Long experience had taught him that her tact, her intuition were infallible in such matters.' Not for nothing did he once refer to 'her portion of our joint duties'.

But Palmerston was now working at an even greater pace than normal and Emily complained, 'I see nothing of him.' Except at the weekends, he hardly ever dined at home, preferring to eat at 3 p.m. and then go straight to the House, jogging on horseback down Piccadilly, wearing his familiar white hat. He seldom returned before 1 a.m. and then 'he never comes to bed till four or five o'clock'.

In some ways, therefore, it came as a welcome respite when in 1858 Palmerston's first ministry foundered over the Orsini Affair. Even Lady Palmerston's wifely ambitions were tempered by the thought that, 'We shall be much more comfortable and more happy when you are out of office, and we have more time to enjoy ourselves . . . I am very glad also,' she could not help adding, 'that you have had no time to bring in a Reform Bill.'

She was less content when Palmerston seized this opportunity to visit France. For her, at 72, such a journey was unthinkable, but nevertheless she still felt young enough to regret being left behind.

On Palmerston's return they retired peaceably to Broadlands but before long Emily had embarked on a round of shooting parties. Borthwick, editor of the *Morning Post*, was a frequent visitor, as was Delane, his colleague on *The Times*. Emily was shrewd enough to be on excellent terms with the press. Palmerston, now 74, wore out the unfortunate United States emissary by tramping after pheasants for over five hours. A junior politician was amazed at the relaxed atmosphere, particularly when Poodle Byng, former intimate of the Prince Regent, gossiped scurrilously about Palmerston's past affairs. Every visitor had to suffer the effects of their host's chronic unpunctuality. Even the Queen was once kept waiting for a drive. Palmerston was invariably late for official functions and it was customary at London dinner parties for the Palmerstons to miss the soup. On one occasion, a guest invited to dine with them arrived to find Palmerston leaving for a ride in Rotten Row.

The respite from politics was a brief one. In June 1859, Palmerston became Prime Minister again. This second ministry was comparatively uneventful, a peaceful postscript to the many storms of his political career. He was now 75 and he would die in Downing Street. Already Emily's diary reflected her anxiety over his health and especially her dread that he would fail or falter in the House. Later she admitted that had this strain continued indefinitely, it would have taken its toll on her own life.

Meanwhile their social engagements gradually dwindled as all Palmerston's flagging energies were concentrated on his great office. Ashley, now Lord Shaftesbury, wrote that he 'retained it from principle and patriotism. Ambition and the love of office had entirely vanished.' Palmerston's younger opponents mocked his dyed whiskers, calling him 'an old painted pantaloon'. But as the friends of their youth died, he found comfort and companionship in Emily. Their life together was a rather solitary one now.

But there was plenty left to do. In 1861, Palmerston was made Warden of the Cinque Ports and Emily went gleefully to explore his official residence, Walmer Castle. 'I am sure you will be delighted,' she reported back. 'The sea is covered with shipping and a beautiful setting sun to light them up.' She was then spending a great deal of time managing her vast properties. In 1862 she paid a lengthy visit to her 'Scotland Estates'.

She was now a dignified and stately old lady, the imposing *grande dame* of the Whig party although still with her old vivacity and her capacity to shock. In 1860 her outspokenness over the abolition of paper duties earned the disapproval of several leading Whigs.

Nor was Palmerston about to subside into unremarked anonymity. In 1863, aged over 80, he found himself cited in a divorce case. The lady in question was the wife of an Irish radical journalist who claimed £20,000 damages before even going to court. Palmerston laughed when the writ was served on him and Lady Palmerston discussed it gaily with her friends. The case was dismissed and Palmerston completely vindicated but nevertheless for weeks London society had talked of nothing else. It was a comment on his reputation that such a charge was even possible and must have been more of an ordeal for Emily than she would ever stoop to admit.

There was one further trial to face. In 1864 Bismarck's troops invaded Denmark and when Palmerston did nothing, the opposition introduced a vote of censure. The news of a government victory was not announced in the House till well after midnight, when Palmerston bounded up to the Ladies' Gallery and his gratified wife. 'What pluck,' observed Disraeli, 'to mount those dreadful stairs at three o'clock in the morning, and eighty years of age.'

He had already had one serious breakdown, during the cold winter of 1861. Now, in November 1864, he suffered another relapse but recovered with the coming of spring. It was the forthcoming winter the doctors rightly feared the most. On 12 October 1865, he developed a violent fever and was expected to die in the night. Once again he managed to rally and even called for port and mutton chops for breakfast but his improvement was only fleeting; this time it was the end. Emily's diary admitted as much: 'I can write no more.'

He died on 18 October 1865, two days before his eighty-fifth birthday. He was still Prime Minister of England: a half finished letter was found in his despatch box. He was buried, at the cabinet's insistence, after a state funeral, in Westminster Abbey, although he would have preferred the peace of Romsey Abbey near the Broadlands estate. Afterwards, Emily returned alone to Brocket, filled as it was with the ghosts of those she had loved. Ironically, on the one occasion she really had need of her daughters, they were travelling abroad and could offer no comfort. Instead she wrote to them from Brocket: 'It has been so dreary and wet here, and I feel oh! so restless and the days so long. I have had many kind letters but I have not the heart to answer them. How much I wish we had some sympathising person to read and pray with us, and lift one's heart up from all this misery . . . that we are passing through . . . I feel so *utterly* wretched.'

And still the letters and tributes poured in. Mrs Disraeli wrote a typically self-effacing letter affirming that, 'Mr Disraeli had a great regard for Lord Palmerston.' Gladstone's, inevitably, was couched in extravagant rhetoric. The Queen who had warmed to Palmerston after he persuaded the House to make Albert Prince Consort, was suitably gracious although less honest than she was in her diary. 'Strange,' she wrote there, 'to think of that strong determined man, with so much worldly ambition – gone!' The press printed eulogies, the Dean of Westminster preached a memorial sermon but to a prostrated Lady Palmerston none of it was any help. She had lost the mainspring of her life.

In time Emily's essentially sanguine nature reasserted itself. In February 1868 she gave up the Piccadilly mansion and settled at 21, Park Lane in a house bought from Edward Bulwer. She was still handsome, still lively, still intensely interested in her surroundings. She would discuss Gladstone's bill to disestablish the Irish Church, which she keenly disapproved of, with all the passion of her youth.

In 1867 she lost her last lifelong friend, Lady Jersey. Lady Holland had died more than twenty years earlier, leaving Emily her fans and Melbourne's portrait by Landseer. Instead, she chose to surround herself with young people, particularly her grandson, Jocelyn, to whom she would read *The Times*. The politics of Gladstone and Disraeli were alien to her but she could still enjoy a vigorous political debate, sitting bolt upright in her airy drawing-room, her cheeks carefully rouged under her black-ribboned cap.

Her last illness only lasted a fortnight. She died peacefully on 11 September 1869 and was buried, appropriately, in Westminster Abbey, near Pitt and alongside her husband.

Lady John Russell

In 1868 Lord John Russell retired after fifty-five years in politics, forty-eight of them in the House of Commons. As a seasoned crusader on the left wing of the Whig party, he should have been able to take credit for many important reforms. Instead, historians have consistently criticized his premiership. His legislative achievements were outweighed by his disastrous failure as a leader of men.

His contemporaries blamed his failure upon the disastrous influence of his second wife, the former Lady Fanny Elliot. 'Deadly Nightshade', they nicknamed her. Anyone less deadly on first acquaintance would have been hard to find in nineteenth-century society. Fanny was a shy, earnest girl who blushed when meeting strangers. She was once overcome with embarrassment on being asked to choose a drink. However, her rather irritating coyness and air of fragility concealed a will of steel.

In politics she was governed by a deeply religious, Presbyterian morality. She saw every issue in black or white. Far more radical than her husband, she had a horror of political compromise. Politics she saw as simply a matter of following your own conscience. For her own part, she entered marriage with various fixed political ideals, among them, electoral reform, justice for

Ireland and the abolition of the crippling tax on corn. Anything else was irrelevant, especially the personalities in the cabinet. She once said she did not see the need for chancellors and budgets.

While this made Fanny admirably progressive in outlook, it did not make for good leadership on the part of her husband. For he *did* listen to her. Almost always armed with a formidable sense of her own rightness, on certain issues Fanny could be inflexible. In addition Lord John's defects of character made him over-susceptible and vacillating. He was weak enough to be led, not only by his forceful wife but also by her rather nondescript father.

Much of Lady John's unwordly outlook derived from her vehemently Protestant childhood. The second daughter of the Whig Earl of Minto, she was brought up in the beautiful, remote Scottish borders where a parcel of books from London was a rare and welcome event. Minto House stood unprotected above a steep, wooded glen in the teeth of what Fanny called 'a *real* Minto wind'. To the end of her life, Fanny loved this wild and beautiful place, and although she was comfortable enough in London, Scotland was always home. As a child she was free to roam the glorious surrounding countryside – fishing in 'Teviot's tide', talking to her friends, the shepherds, in the Cheviot hills, or scrambling among the rocks of Minto crags below the nesting falcons.

The enforced isolation made Fanny shy and serious. Her father's library appealed to her more than making new friends. She was still in her teens when she wrote of her sister, that she was 'just the age I began to be unhappy because I began to think'. If she had begun to laugh, she would have made herself more popular, but Fanny never had much of a sense of humour. Ponderous puns were the nearest she got to joking. Her idea of madcap merriment was a stately Scottish country dance.

And now she could no longer retreat to the familiar seclusion of Minto for in 1835, her father was appointed to the Admiralty. For Fanny it meant not just a move to London but London society: breakfast parties at the Duchess of Buccleuch's – 'my horror of breakfasts is only increased by having been to this one'; luncheon in the grounds of Holland House, where Lady Holland sat in state with a page in dark green uniform behind her chair; dinners, suppers, assemblies and endless balls.

'I wonder what it is that makes one sometimes like and sometimes dislike balls,' she wrote in her diary in March 1836. 'I am sure it is not . . . from love of admiration that one is fond of them . . . I sometimes wish I was pretty. And I do not think it is a very foolish wish: it would give me courage to be agreeable.' Later on, when her hatred of London became insupportable, it would be society that was so 'tiresome'. But for the moment she pondered earnestly on her defects. 'I dislike myself more than ever. How sad it is to appear to everyone different from what one is.' In the summers there would be the blessed escape to Scotland. 'Oh for the boys and guns and dogs, a heathery moor, and a blue Scotch heaven above me!'

On one such holiday in 1840, Lord John Russell, then Colonial Secretary, was a visitor. Fanny's reaction, in a letter to her brother, was tinged with awe. 'We have done our best to make his time pass less heavily . . . with a set of stupid unpolitical ladies like ourselves . . .' She added that Lord John seemed in 'very bad *political* spirits'. It was far more than that, as she would soon discover.

Lord John had been a frequent visitor to his cabinet colleague in the Admiralty. The hero of the Reform Bill had become a family friend. On his first wife's death in 1838, his loneliness was plainly visible, and Fanny, with her ever-hungry conscience, was moved by the sight. In her diary she mourned 'the sad, sad news . . . of Lady John Russell. God give strength to her poor unhappy husband and watch over his dear little motherless children.' She tried to play her part by inviting all six of them to Putney, where they romped in the garden, occasionally with Lord John. More often he joined Minto and Palmerston in informal cabinet meetings after dinner and Fanny would sit and listen while they talked 'war with France till bedtime'. To her he was unquestionably her father's friend, although she admired him more than anyone else politically. Certainly there was no physical attraction at this stage and probably never was to be.

Tiny and frail – he was only 8 stone and 5 foot 4¾ inches – Lord John had been notoriously unsuccessful with women. Before marrying his first wife, he had proposed to several others, including his own future sister-in-law and Lady Palmerston's daughter, Minnie Cowper. His weak frame was continually racked by colds and hayfever. He would feel faint if he encountered 'hot rooms, late hours and bad air'. As a result, his brother's sage advice to him was that, 'You are a man of settled pursuits and habits and must have a wife that will take an interest in them – a gadding, flirting, dressing, ball-going wife would be the Devil.'

Lady Fanny was definitely not that. Moreover, she was intelligent, conscientious and progressive-minded, better-read and far more knowledgeable politically than most of her female contemporaries. At twenty-four, she was slim and sprightly with dark hair, brown eyes and appealing freckles. Despite the fact that he was twice her age, Lord John determined to propose.

To Fanny it came as a bolt from the blue, to find on the morning of their guest's departure, a letter from him asking her to be his wife. 'I see it . . . but yet I do not believe it . . .' she wrote to her sister, and to her brother, 'I suppose he did not at all know what he was doing.'

Lord John received a polite note of refusal, much to Lord and Lady Minto's relief. Lord Minto commented that he had never thought of his friend as old until this proposal to his daughter. But over the next nine months, as Fanny gradually changed her mind, her parents, too, became reconciled to the match.

Lord John's next letter did much to help his cause, especially his description of his 'wretched state of misery . . . [which] leaves me to hope that my life may not be long'. If he needed another advocate, he had one in his sister-in-law, Harriet Lister, who frequently reminded Fanny that he was 'unequalled in all the world'. Back in London he showed himself to be thoughtful and sensitive, doing everything possible to spare her embarrassment or pain. Nevertheless, the press buzzed with rumours which played on Fanny's old doubts about her sociability. 'What a stone I am,' she confided to her diary. 'The more I think . . . the more I bewilder myself.' Significantly, she now could not stop thinking about him. His name crops up in every letter, usually emphatically underlined.

Her twenty-fifth birthday fell in November 1840. For the first time, she felt time running out. 'It frightens me to be twenty-five,' she mused in her diary, and then, with seeming resignation in a letter: 'It is hard . . . that a woman should be considered so far down the hill at 25, when a man at 27 is only reaching the top.' A few months later she was telling her mother that she felt too old to be 'desperately in love'. Lady Minto was inclined to agree with her. She had been won over by a visit from Lord John himself. '[I was] *horribly* frightened, as I hate lovers . . .' As an obedient daughter, Fanny was reassured by her approval. She had also begun to worry about Lord John's motherless children, four by his wife's first marriage and two of his own. Perhaps they needed her? Perhaps it was a vocation? Both ideas appealed to her pious sense of duty.

By April 1841, Lord John sensed that she was wavering and cleverly let her reach a decision alone. He hardly saw her until a June party at Lady Palmerston's. Four days later they were engaged.

Fanny's letters show a mood of contented resignation. She called herself coyly, 'a poor weak but happy child'. Most of her thoughts were centred on the 'dear precious children' and she seldom mentions her emerald engagement ring or her husband-to-be. She does, however, record that she could not call him John. 'I find even Lord John difficult enough as yet.'

With such a start the marriage could have been a disaster. Bertrand Russell, Fanny's grandson, blamed her 'puritan inhibitions'. It was also likely that the appearance of her 48 year-old ailing husband did not appeal to Fanny's sexuality. However, in their common love of literature and politics, they had a basis for companionship if not passion. To Fanny her husband's career was a sacred duty and her interest in it never flagged.

The marriage took place in the drawing-room at Minto after a frantic check by Lord John that the Scottish ceremony was legal. The day before, 19 July 1841, was, Fanny noted sadly, 'My last . . . as a child of Minto.' But they spent their honeymoon in her beloved Scotland for the Duchess of Buccleuch had lent them Bowhill. Afterwards they returned to Lord John's home in Wilton Crescent. At first Fanny thought it a 'strange' house but her sense of insecurity in it disappeared after her husband broached the subject of his first wife who had lived there. Gentle and fond of flowers, she had been as fair as Fanny was dark – a tiny china-doll figure of a woman. Already a widow when she married, she had been used to a retiring life, devoting much of her time to needlework and sketching. Ten days after the birth of her daughter, she died as quietly and unobtrusively as she had lived. No woman could have offered a greater contrast to Fanny.

At the end of August 1841, several weeks after their election defeat in July, the Whig government finally resigned. Sir Robert Peel, the new Prime Minister, had been kept waiting a month to take over until Lord John returned from Bowhill. The transfer of power completed, the Russells went to Endsleigh, near Tavistock, the Duke of Bedford's house in a gentle Devon valley. Lady Minto felt that it would 'cement' their marriage, and Fanny saw it as a chance 'to know one another in a quiet home life'. Her delight that her husband was out of office was rather ominous in view of the future. In five years' time he would be Prime Minister and there would be no time for 'quiet and old gowns'. But for the moment there was plenty and Fanny made the most of it, riding, rambling and studying botany or reading aloud to her husband.

It was just as well. Her next few years were dogged by illness, precipitated by an attack of typhus in 1843. After the birth of her first son a year earlier she was to suffer several miscarriages. Interminable months were spent resting, gathering her strength 'for the great squeezes, wch were necessary but not agreeable'.

Lord John was a patient, solicitous husband. He sent her cheering little notes in rhyme or dog-Latin. On his 51st birthday she repaid him with a long, earnest poem, entitled in all seriousness, 'O father of my baby boy!' Like her mother who was constantly composing border 'ballads', Lady John considered herself a passable poet. Fortunately for her peace of mind her poems were mostly read by her family, and so she was never brought to task for them.

In the meantime, ill though she was, 'a broken-down,

useless bit of rubbish' as she once called herself pathetically, she could still bring influence to bear. The affair of the 'Edinburgh letter' was a case in point. Although Lord John drafted this surprise attack on Peel's government, Lady John, then in Edinburgh, sent it to be published and her husband read it for the first time in print. The letter could have been written by Lady John herself. It voiced a view dear to her heart, namely that Peel and his Cabinet were being criminally slow in taking steps to lower the price of corn. Such an unexpectedly extreme statement from a well-known Whig in the midst of the delicate Corn Law negotiations, caused Melbourne acute political embarrassment. Peel resigned, but had to return when the Whigs could not form a government. Lord John himself suffered in the 'lame and mournful' mess. Queen Victoria thought, as a result of it, that 'Lord John . . . never *can* be Prime Minister for he has not a shadow of authority.'

But Fanny, who, for much of the time, did not want to see him Prime Minister in any case, for it would have necessitated him leaving her side, was 'delighted that the chief barrier between him and the Radical part of the Whig party should be knocked down . . . It is what I have long wished.' Her ideals were intact. That was what mattered to her. For the rest, she did not shrink from burdening him with worries about her health, even hinting that she had not long to live. As a result, at the height of the crisis, Lord John had three agonized, sleepless nights. It was partly anxiety for his wife that persuaded him to give up trying to form a government. No wonder Spencer Walpole, Lord John's biographer, called Fanny privately, 'The Influence'.

She also interfered on behalf of her own family. Elliots held sway in every sort of official post. That they did so was not so much shameless nepotism as Fanny's naïve belief in their merit. In fact, they were a mediocre family and their preferment might well have damaged Lord John. There was a general fear that he might 'over-Elliot' a future government.

But some Elliots were sensible. Her mother worried about Fanny's unsociableness, particularly when she alienated the formidable Lady Holland. Fanny hated fashion. She was loath to have dinner parties and tried to entertain informally, serving tea in ordinary day-clothes from 9 to 11 to the astonishment of London society.

Partly, she felt swamped by her great responsibilities. Seven children were a heavy burden for a girl in her twenties with a husband too busy to do more than offer perfunctory advice. 'You think I did not know what I was undertaking,' she wrote in a rare mood of bitterness to her mother, 'and you are right.' Nevertheless, the children loved her. She had a childlike simplicity that made it easy for her to enter their world.

But her unworldliness was not exactly an asset for housekeeping and Fanny was never to be a good manager. Eventually, her father came to the rescue and sent down servants from the family estate. 'She does not believe,' he said paternally, 'that there is anybody in the world so wicked as really to intend to cheat, or to overcharge.'

By now the family had moved from Wilton Crescent to a house they had built in Chesham Place. The site, given to them by the Duke of Bedford, was largely reclaimed marshland. Lord John could remember shooting snipe there as a boy. It had been drained after a cholera epidemic had decimated nearby Eaton Place. Their new home was a comfortable town residence with an oak staircase fit for a country house. Fanny, who like Lady Peel loved gardening, planted yellow jasmine and creepers for the walls. But there was no Clean Air Act and 'smuts and dust at last prevailed'. She was never fond of Chesham Place. 'Oh, why, why, do people not all live in the country?'

In 1846 Peel resigned as Prime Minister. On a beautiful June day the Queen sent for Lord John Russell, now almost 54. The country was not with him and there were cruel cartoons in the newspapers and magazines such as *Punch*. His wife, however, urged him on: it was nothing less than his duty to become 'the head of the most moral and religious government ever'. She would brook no compromise. 'All I care about,' she once said, 'is that you should do what is most right in the sight of God.'

Already, she had made her views felt over the Irish Coercion Bill, which she was convinced would only further embitter the Irish. Lord John, who had thought privately that stricter laws might possibly reduce the crime rate, was persuaded to press for more conciliatory measures. In doing so he contributed to Peel's fall and so, indirectly, to his own premiership.

Although it began surprisingly well, it was ultimately an unsuccessful ministry. Lord John, wilful, capricious, forever unsure of himself, vacillated between the Cabinet, his brother and his wife. Towards the end of his period in office there was a discernible decline in his ability; the last few months were marked by mislaid papers and neglected business. The Queen complained of his unhelpful reports to her and the Cabinet was fragmented, on the verge of a total split.

Lord John's worst dispute was with Lord Palmerston, his Foreign Secretary, whose authoritarian attitude led to continuous friction. The Queen, in particular, was pressing for Palmerston to be replaced. In December 1851 Lord John compromised by dismissing but defending him, an unsatisfactory solution which led, the following year, to the fall of the ministry. Even Lord John's attempts to conciliate Palmerston were in vain. Lady Palmerston talked of 'treachery' and barred the Russells from her parties. Lady John was not much help.

She despised 'the plausibilities of commonplace politicians. I open my Bible at night. It is going from darkness into light.'

To be fair, she was still weak and depressed by illness and childbirth. She tormented herself with fits of soul-searching, for once omitting to be coy. 'I am cold, dull and unworthy of such a husband,' she concluded during one of these. On another occasion, her high ideals forgotten, she wrote wretchedly to her sister-in-law: 'We must buy every great blessing at a great price, that of children perhaps the greatest . . . you and I have often lamented together over the loss of our *care*less days – in short we have wished to shake ourselves free of husbands and children . . .' It was a much more human side to her that emerged on these occasions than when she was on her moral high horse.

Lord John meanwhile had his own problems. He was having difficulty in making ends meet. In 1850 he told a committee of the House of Commons that the premiership had led him into debt. His brother, the vastly rich Duke of Bedford, could have rescued him, but he was notoriously mean. Lord John's election expenses were paid, but further requests were met with ill grace and a homily on the perils of extravagance. In fact, Lord John lived very modestly, but as Prime Minister he had a position to uphold. Downing Street was dingy and ill-equipped for entertaining. He was in urgent need of a country home.

Eventually, when the Duke of Bedford did nothing, the Queen felt compelled to step into the breach. In March 1847 she offered the Russells Pembroke Lodge in Richmond Park. It was a homely, rambling house in an old-fashioned garden with a famous view. Lady John, relieved to be able to contemplate the spires of London from a distance, set to work with a will – planting a rose-garden, hanging the prints that were a gift from the

Queen, watching out for possible economies with an eagle eye. She even cut one end off a sofa to make it fit. Busier and happier than she had been for many years, she wrote to her sister that she wished time could stand still. And Lord John, too, was enjoying rural life. 'He rides and walks and drinks ale and grows fat.' To complete the image of a country squire, he kept two heifers and some poultry in a paddock. Typically, the venture failed: 'When well fatted . . . [they] were too old to be eaten.'

Both Fanny and Lord John contrived to be at Pembroke Lodge as much as possible – always at weekends, and sometimes also in midweek. 'Up and downers', they called their enforced stays at Chesham Place and dreaded the moment when the Queen's messenger called, heralding a return to London. It was quite a cavalcade. Lord John would set off after breakfast in a light, racy brougham, with the family following in a rather more sedate carriage. The luggage would come last, piled high in a carrier's cart. In the summer Lord John frequently rode back from the House, or else his horse would be brought to Hammersmith Bridge, escorted by all the children old enough to ride. Lady John, meanwhile, watched anxiously from a nearby hill.

Not surprisingly, their social life suffered. For a Prime Minister, Lord John entertained dangerously little. And while Fanny continued to plead his need of rest and fresh, country air, discontent among the backbenchers grew ominously strong. 'Johnny has come to dwell in a Wigwam,' wrote Joseph Parkes, and indeed he seemed totally cut off from the main body of his supporters. During the session in London, Lady John did try to entertain but there were complaints that her assemblies were full of 'Diplomats and Elliots', by this time often one and the same thing. There was also talk about the frugal, nursery food. The Earl of Carlisle, visiting

Richmond in 1851, scoffed at 'a most simple and primitive ménage: we had no dinner, but tea at 8 with a boiled chicken'. High tea with toast and jam was an innovation of Fanny's which she served unconcernedly even when foreign royalty were guests. Lord John never questioned her. Neither of them cared about food.

However, the more worldly members of the Russell family were shocked at Fanny's lack of social graces. Her step-daughter compared her with the hospitable Lady Palmerston. 'She [Lady Palmerston] was a real help to her husband in his political life. Politics and society, she blended with the greatest ease and success, wielding them for her husband's cause . . .' The inference is clear. Lady Palmerston herself was used to Lady John's ungregariousness. She contented herself with playing hostess to Fanny's young step-daughters, saying resignedly, 'Well, I suppose it is of no use sending a card to Lady John.' Instead, she shrewdly appealed to Fanny's conscience by asking her to call on her brother Melbourne, ill at Brocket.

Fanny would have avoided visiting the Palmerstons in any case. She disapproved of Lord Palmerston whom she thought immoral, and she disliked 'clever' political gossip of the sort practised by 'regular hardened lady politicians' like his wife. 'I care very much for the questions themselves,' she wrote, 'but grow wearied to death of all the details and personalities . . . and the conversation of lady politicians, made up as it is of these . . . The more interested I am in the thing itself, the more angry I am with the nonsense they talk about and had rather listen to the most humdrum domestic twaddle.'

In fact, the conversation at Pembroke Lodge was far from humdrum. Lord John's many literary friends saw to that. And Lady Fanny who had dutifully waded through the greater part of English literature, could hold her own with Samuel Rogers, Dickens, Tennyson and Froude. Pembroke Lodge was open house on summer Sundays, and sometimes over forty visitors arrived for tea. If they were wise, they avoided dinner, for Fanny was an inveterate games player with a huge repertoire culled from Minto to inflict on unwary guests. Thackeray escaped by offering to read his latest work. Like Dickens he published his novels in monthly instalments, as serials.

In 1849 Fanny's second son was born, shortly before Lord John's fifty-seventh birthday. The Russells celebrated with a fête at Pembroke Lodge, where the children from the village school they had founded, danced underneath the trees. By now Fanny's brood of Russell step-children were almost all adult, although with Presbyterian zeal she tried to keep them 'fresh and innocent and unworldly . . . I am not over-fond of experience'. She was horrified when nineteen-year-old Adelaide drew political cartoons of Ireland. Politics were not a fitting subject for a pure, untouched girl, although she herself had revelled in them when young. In the circumstances the children grew up surprisingly normal and unaffected by their suffocatingly religious background. Nevertheless, at four her own son, Johnny, was heard to wonder why monks thought God preferred them not to speak.

In February 1852 Lord John's tottering ministry finally collapsed. In the turmoil that followed only one thing was clear – Lord John could never unite the Whig party. He could have retired with his reputation comparatively intact. Instead, reluctant to hand over to Palmerston and spurred on by his ambitious wife, he went, as Clarendon noted sardonically, 'knocking on every man's door . . . in obedience to Lady John's mandate . . . in total forgetfulness of his own dignity'. In spite of his efforts, in December 1852, when a Peelite-Whig coalition did return to power, Lord John was not at the head of it. Lady John was outraged that her husband could have been passed over for Lord Aberdeen, that 'solemn old Athenian pet', whom, she suspected, the Queen had 'long wished to see at the head of all things'.

Her disappointment, however, was not all for her rejected husband. On the contrary, she dreaded the ministerial despatch boxes, which had increased six-fold since 1828. But there were her ideals to consider and the cause of electoral reform. In power, Lord John could be prevailed upon to 'purify and reform much that is morally wrong – much that you would not tolerate in your own household'. In support of this simple political creed she was prepared to risk his career. When Aberdeen offered Lord John the Foreign Office, she proposed instead that he led the House, with a seat in the Cabinet but no office to tie him down. 'Thus,' she wrote vaguely to her father, 'he will have time to care for the general concern, to work at Reform, Education &c . . . [it] is both *grander* and more useful . . . [he] can undertake a responsibility greater than if he was really Prime Minister.' She was much encouraged when a hint from Aberdeen about his retirement brought this goal into sight. But she had reckoned without the Cabinet who vetoed her suggestion. Lord John was forced to accept the Foreign Office or nothing. Bitterly, Fanny criticized his colleagues for 'grumbling behind his back', being 'contemptuous' and 'obstructive'. In the next few months, she more than earned her nickname, 'Deadly Nightshade', inflaming Cabinet suspicions to such an extent that Gladstone doubted afterwards, 'if there is any man in England . . . who could have borne what he has had to bear from Lady John'.

Most difficult of all for her husband, was Fanny's feud with Queen Victoria. She blamed her openly for much of Lord John's trouble. Admittedly, the fault was on both sides: the fertile Queen mocked Fanny's difficulties in giving birth. But the Russells brought the quarrel into the open by refusing to go to Balmoral. 'Stand *I* will not,' declared Fanny before a visit to Windsor in 1853, 'even at the risk of her thinking me lazy or affected, one of wch epithets . . . she applies to every woman less strong than herself.' The Queen had her revenge by refusing to house their new-born daughter, Agatha. '*No room* for Baby in Windsor Cottage!' Fanny wrote indignantly to her sister. More seriously, Victoria turned against Lord John politically. Even Palmerston was preferable to 'selfish, peevish Johnny'.

It was a difficult time for Lord John. In 1853 he resigned as Foreign Secretary and remained in the Cabinet without office. The following year, his attempt to put up a new Reform Bill met with strong opposition, and he withdrew it to save Aberdeen's already tottering government. Fanny was furious. Despairingly she wondered how she could bring up her children in such a cowardly, selfish world. Worse was to follow. Her husband now resigned the Lord Presidency of the Council, took office under Palmerston and resigned that too, following criticism of his diplomacy at the exploratory peace negotiations at Vienna. He was in a state bordering on nervous collapse. 'Blood, Blood,' he kept repeating during the long nights when he could not sleep. For nearly four years Russell remained out of office, until in 1859 he began his second term as Foreign Secretary, under Palmerston. He was 67.

This time, ironically, it was his wife who had persuaded him into it, eager for him to embrace yet another cause – that of a united Italy. When the Anglo-Italian Sir James Lacaita came to plead for aid, it was Fanny, the 'Italianissima', he asked to see, even pushing past her maid to visit her in bed upstairs.

By 1861 Lord John was tired, although he had leaned

heavily on Palmerston for support. 'The two terrible old men', Queen Victoria called them. She was now semi-reconciled to her Foreign Secretary and in 1861 created him Earl Russell. With the title, at last, came a kind of peace. Gladstone emerged as the new force behind the Liberal party and Russell spent much of the remainder of his time as Foreign Secretary in the safe confines of Pembroke Lodge. Even Fanny had ceased to take notice of the outside world. It was only the fate of the Irish – 'lovable, lovely, sorrowful Ireland' – that could light the spark of her former passion. Otherwise, 'Our happiness is chiefly in the past,' she wrote, 'and present in this world, in memory more than hope.'

As she grew older, her puritan scruples multiplied. She condemned the 'rackety life of a London butterfly . . . for *any* girl'. Society came to pity poor Agatha, the only girl among her four children, who lived, unmarried and sequestered, behind Pembroke Lodge's high walls. According to her step-sister, Georgiana, married to Julia Peel's nephew, it was like 'a hermitage'. If it was a hermitage, it was a pleasant one, and Russell still entertained *his* friends. Palmerston came often now, eating enormously, and evidently concentrating more on his food than on talking. Jowett discussed history and philosophy in the long, light study overlooking the garden. Later they dined in a room decorated like a garden, with a trellis and leafy wallpaper.

It was not altogether a political wilderness. Under the spur of his wife's incessant prompting, the Irish question came to occupy Lord Russell more and more. On Palmerston's death, he led one more short-lived ministry from November 1865 to February 1866, but his energy was flagging and little was achieved. 'Sad, most sad to me,' mourned Fanny, 'that his enjoyments, his active powers, yearly dwindle . . . alas for the days of his vigour.' It was more difficult for her than for most wives: she herself was still in her prime.

The end was probably hastened by a series of personal tragedies, as first one son, then another, fell incurably ill. In 1876, their eldest son died in the Welsh mansion where two years before, he had lost his wife and daughter. The surviving grandchild, the young Bertrand Russell, came to live with Fanny at Richmond. From the start he disliked his stern-principled grandmother and would hide from her among the trees in the garden.

She was a lonely figure as she nursed her husband in his old age. He had been almost her only friend for nearly forty years. She missed his companionship and their daily strolls in the garden when she longed for 'lakes and mountains and liberty out of my reach'. But inevitably, his illnesses became longer and more debilitating until when Gladstone came, he saw only 'a noble wreck'. He died in 1878 on a calm May evening, holding his wife's hand, and saying he was 'quite ready to go'. Immediately, the offer came of a Westminster Abbey funeral but he was buried as he had wished in the Russell family vault at Chenies.

In her distress Fanny clung to her familiar surroundings, terrified in case the Queen reclaimed Pembroke Lodge. 'Oh the blessing of being still able to call it home,' she wrote almost joyfully when the message came to stay. In 1892 she took a house in Hindhead, where the heath reminded her of her beloved Scotland. Afterwards, she returned to Richmond and did not leave it for the rest of her life.

She had plenty of interests still to occupy her, 'treasures beyond price . . . left to my old age'. Reading had been the habit of a lifetime. In the past she had read aloud to her husband; now she read voraciously alone: Milton, Wordsworth, Wesley, Burns, her favourite poet, and *David Copperfield*, which made her cry. Until she was very old she rose before dawn to read theological works. But organized religion she had always shunned. 'I make my church in the garden.' Her last engagement, in Richmond, was the opening of a new *Free* Church.

Long before the end, she could sense death approaching and, typically, wrote a poem, as she had on every other important occasion in her life. Gladstone was one of her last and most faithful visitors and she would eagerly await him to hear news of Ireland, almost her only political interest now. He found her physically frail but mentally lively, her brown eyes darting inquisitively under her white lace cap.

In 1898 she died, surrounded by her children and grandchildren. In many ways it was a relief: cloistered and protected though she was, she had found the modern world increasingly alien.

Mrs Disraeli

When Benjamin Disraeli first met Mary Anne Wyndham Lewis, on an April evening in 1832, she was already forty and the wife of a Member of Parliament. Disraeli, twelve years younger and just returned from his travels in the East, was the centre of attention at a lavish party given by his friend and fellow novelist, Edward Bulwer. Dressed exotically as always (he normally wore a velvet coat and vivid waistcoat), his ringlets flowing over his long lace ruffles and festooned from head to foot with chains and rings, he had all the ladies clamouring to meet him. And one of the most insistent as he later wrote to his sister, Sarah, was 'Mrs Wyndham Lewis, a pretty little woman, a flirt and a rattle; indeed gifted with a volubility I should think unequalled and of which I can convey no idea. She told me that she liked "silent melancholy men". I answered that I had no doubt of it.'

But after two or three meetings he had begun to find her tiresome. At one house where he was asked to escort her into dinner, his reply was, 'Oh, anything rather than that insufferable woman,' then, 'putting his thumbs into the armholes of his waistcoat he walked up to her and offered her his arm.' And in the circumstances this was only to be expected. Many people found this tiny, talkative, over-dressed woman, still girlish in spite of her age, slightly ridiculous. To an ambitious and cultivated young novelist she must have seemed empty-headed if not stupid. Disraeli himself admitted later that she could never remember who came first, the Greeks or the Romans, and her blunders were already legendary, especially her remark about the great Dean Swift. 'Who is this Dr Swift? Can I ask him to my parties?'

To be fair to Mary Anne she was not brought up as Disraeli was in a household of 25,000 books. Her father's family were Devon farmers; her mother had some distant relatives who were landed gentry and a brother who was a major-general under Wellington, but they were never anything but respectably middle-class. However, it was an exceptionally happy childhood. Mary Anne was known by a series of affectionate pet-names like 'Whizzy' and 'Tiddy', and later on she admitted that, as a child, she had never been crossed.

In 1793, when Mary Anne was two, her father, Lieutenant John Evans, died at sea. Her mother married again several years later and they went to live at Clifton near Bristol, close to Hotwell Springs spa and a great centre for fashionable society. The Evans family was welcomed, probably because of Mrs Evans's rich relations, and Mary Anne was soon besieged by suitors. She had grown very pretty with huge blue eyes in an oval face, a graceful neck and glossy brown hair. She was small and slim and fond of wearing frills and lace. But much of her appeal lay in her personality. Mary Anne chattered and laughed her way through every party, flirting first with one admirer, then another. Yet under her feather-brained exterior there was real warmth and a vein of kindly shrewdness.

In 1815 when she was twenty-three, she was introduced at a ball to an eccentric bachelor of thirty-five called Wyndham Lewis. He immediately fell hopelessly in love with her and wrote her ardent verses to prove it, with such lines as:

'On flow'ry banks, by ev'ry murmuring stream,
Mary Anne is my Muse's softest theme . . .
Dear lovely girl, I cry to all around,
Dear lovely girl, the flattering vales resound.'

In spite of the abominable poetry and Wyndham Lewis's reputation for being rather odd, Mary Anne decided to marry him. He was eligible and came from an old Welsh landed family while Mary Anne had little money and a lazy, extravagant brother whom she adored and who had always looked to her to settle his debts.

In fact, the marriage seems to have gone rather well. Wyndham Lewis prospered in the iron trade and Mary Anne became one of the leading hostesses in South Wales. They rebuilt their house, calling it 'Pantgynlais Castle' and Mary Anne rushed about the country, giving shooting parties for their neighbours, taking people to the races at Worcester, organizing balls at Cardiff. It was all much grander than anything she had been used to and she took rather a naïve pleasure in it. She said of one ball she went to, 'Before I came the people thought I should give myself airs – but they were charmed at my courtesy.' She was genuinely fond of Wyndham Lewis and wrote to her brother, 'My dear Wyndham is kinder and fonder of me than ever. We are hardly ever two hours apart.' He showered her with jewels and dresses, bought her a new carriage and hired a maid and footman to ride with her.

The only arguments they had were over the money she gave to her brother. Apart from paying off John's numerous debts, Mary Anne wanted to buy him promotion in the army, but Wyndham Lewis had already paid out £1300 and quite reasonably refused to go any further. Nevertheless, Mary Anne continued to write to John at least twice a fortnight for twenty years. Before she met Disraeli she probably loved her brother more than anyone and in her letters to him she poured out the great wealth of affection in her nature. 'Is it possible, John, you don't love me . . . the idea sometimes make my heart ready to break.'

In 1820 Wyndham Lewis stood for parliament and Mary Anne became the wife of a politician, something she was to remain for more than fifty years. They bought a fine London house in Grosvenor Gate with two drawing-rooms, four guest and six servants' bedrooms. Mary Anne thought it 'so grand looking'. In 1827 when they moved in Mary Anne gave a ball and wrote to her brother in her usual breathless style, 'My company were most of the first people in London, the Duke of Wellington said it was like fairy land, the best ball he had been at this season, but are you not dazzled at your little Whizzy having received the Noble Hero at her house.' In fact, as she later admitted, Lord and Lady Clarendon had befriended her and 'invited some of the Dukes and Earls'.

She was bound to meet Disraeli sooner or later, especially after she got to know his friends the Bulwers. Rosina Bulwer became her great confidante. They were both lively, both unconventional and considered by a lot of people rather common. But Mary Anne was also warm-hearted and generous where Rosina was not.

She may not have impressed Disraeli but from the start he fascinated her and she was partly instrumental in getting him a seat in parliament. In the general election of 1837 Disraeli was elected for Maidstone along with Wyndham Lewis. Mary Anne, who had campaigned for him indefatigably, rushed to the scene of triumph, in a dress of appropriately vivid blue. 'Mr Disraeli will in a very few years be one of the greatest men of his day . . . They call him my parliamentary protégé,' she wrote significantly to her brother. For his part, Disraeli seems to have recognized her kindness and well-meaning enthusiasm and to have become quite fond of her. Mr and Mrs Lewis went to stay with the Disraeli family at Bradenham and letters passed between them sending 'love, affection and compliments'. They saw each other frequently while parliament was in session and Disraeli and Mary Anne even went to the theatre. Writing afterwards to his sister, Disraeli mentioned several dukes and lords and then added with amusement, 'Mrs W. L., who was very proud, evidently, of being there.'

As the months passed notes flew between Disraeli's lodgings and Grosvenor Gate. He no longer bothered to start 'Dear Mrs Wyndham Lewis' and simply signed himself D or Dis. This easy friendship might have continued indefinitely but in 1838 something happened which drastically altered their lives. Wyndham Lewis, now aged sixty, died suddenly of a heart attack in Mary Anne's presence.

In the last few months of their marriage Mary Anne had taken him rather for granted. She no longer accompanied him to campaign at elections but stayed in London, flirting with her friends, some of whom were disreputable young rakes, and according to letters found among her papers, making secret assignations with unknown admirers. But now that she had lost her husband, Mary Anne was shocked and stunned. Copying out a verse that reminded her of him, she wrote dejectedly beside it, 'How I miss Whm. I feel like a body without a soul now that he is gone.'

Of course her friends rallied round to cheer her and she turned to Disraeli especially for sympathy and advice with her legal problems. He cheered her with amusing accounts of his doings, signing himself 'Your faithful friend'. Once, when he was invited to a fashionable banquet in the presence of Peel and Wellington, she sent him some of his beloved gold chains. She was delighted when a fellow-guest thought he was to be

Lord Mayor. And when her brother died shortly afterwards, it was Disraeli who would fill this gap too.

She showed just how much she had come to depend on him when she wrote to him from her husband's estate in Wales. 'Upon my honour, dear kind Dizzy, you are the only person I have written to (except on business) since I left town . . . I am glad you pass so much of your time with Lady L . . . because the more you go to there or any other married lady the less likely you are to think of marrying yourself . . . I hate married men . . . I would much sooner you were dead.'

It is not certain when Disraeli first thought of marrying her. Certainly, he had got to a precarious point in his career when a good marriage would have helped enormously. He had never forgotten the advice of Count d'Orsay when he first entered politics. 'You will not make love! You will not intrigue! You have your seat; do not risk anything! If you meet with a widow, then marry.' London society was convinced that he only wanted her money. They could not conceive of any other reason why the 'joyous, fantastic, captivating' Mr Disraeli should tie himself to 'that old woman'. Mary Anne herself obviously planned on remarrying. She had falsified her age on her husband's tombstone, precisely with that in mind. But over Disraeli she had her doubts. She had made him agree to wait a year for an answer. Now her affection cooled slightly. She did not write so often and when she did she complained about him cultivating grand friends. To which Disraeli's characteristic reply was, 'I do not know what you mean by passing "so much" of my time with Lady Londonderry. I do not pass any more time with her than with Lady anybody else.' It culminated in a furious row when Mary Anne threw him out of her house, reminding him that he owed her money and calling him 'a selfish bully'. Disraeli went straight back to his lodgings in Park Street and sat down to write the famous 1500-word letter which made her decide to marry him.

He began by admitting that 'when I first made my advances to you, I was influenced by no romantic feelings'. But he said, he had been touched by her grief for her husband, finding her 'amiable' and 'tender'. As for her fortune, it was much smaller than he or anyone else had thought, in fact not really a fortune at all, merely a life interest in her husband's property. In any case he would soon be financially independent – 'all that society can offer is at my command' – and Mary Anne would be left to regret 'the passionate heart that you have forfeited and the genius you have betrayed'.

And most of this was probably quite sincere. Afterwards Mary Anne joked that when Disraeli married her it was for money, 'but if he had the chance again, he would marry me for love'. In fact she was quite shrewd for all her frivolity, and she could see what few other people saw – that in his brilliant, precarious career, more than anything else Disraeli needed affection and stability. As he said in his letter to her, 'My nature demands that my life shall be perpetual love.' He had always fallen in love with older women and many of his emotional needs were those of a child. Mary Anne gave him total devotion and security, mothered him, protected him and believed absolutely in him. 'Health, my clear brain and your fond love,' he wrote just before his marriage, 'and I feel that I can conquer the world.'

He never thought her stupid. He had seen her good sense and judgement at work for him during the election. And he welcomed her frivolity as a relaxation after the battle of wits most women expected of him. At least in his own home there would always be peace and reassurance. Mary Anne would never try to compete with him. Rather she would live only for him. To be free 'from all the torturing passions of intrigue' he could disregard her social blunders, her lack of style and her undoubted ignorance. The success of their marriage lay in these words of Mary Anne's: 'Every woman in society for years has been taking from Dis. He appreciates better than any man I know the value of a woman who has something to give in return for being given to . . . Now I want to give and I know how most exactly.' Years later after her death Disraeli summed up what was necessary for a happy marriage, 'Sympathy . . . Sympathy goes before beauty or talent. Sympathy – and that is what I have had.'

So Mary Anne's mind was made up. She wrote back to him, 'For God's sake come to me. I never desired you to leave the house or implied or thought a word about money . . . I am devoted to you.' They were married on 28 August 1839 at St George's, Hanover Square and Mary Anne, who was very practical, noted the fact in her accounts book. 'Gloves 2/6. In hand £3000. Married 28.8.1839. Dear Dizzy became my husband.' She also observed with her customary frankness that he seemed 'lost in astonishment' at the thought.

They honeymooned at Tunbridge Wells and on the continent where Mary Anne found Baden-Baden not much better than Cheltenham. Nevertheless, she seemed oblivious of it when she wrote to Disraeli's father. 'We simplify life,' she said. 'First to talk – to eat – to drink – to sleep – love and be loved.'

Disraeli returned to an ordered, domestic life in a fine house in Grosvenor Gate where he could at last entertain as he wanted to. He played his part as the sober young husband by wearing rather less lace and fewer chains. The invitations were not quite so frequent. Mary Anne was not accepted in the highest circles. But in the first few years of their marriage their only real arguments were over money. Disraeli was deeply in debt and tried to hide his difficulties from Mary Anne. She disapproved of his extravagance and got upset when she could not read his letters. But eventually it all came out and it was Mary Anne who saved the situation. Altogether, she paid off about £13,000 for Disraeli and henceforth kept a watchful eye on his finances. Throughout her life, she hated owing money. One of the jottings in her much-thumbed 'Occasion' book read: 'When may a man be said literally to be over head and ears in debt? When he wears a wig that's not paid for.' It was a joke, of course, but at heart she meant it.

With his debts paid and his domestic life organized, Disraeli was free to concentrate on politics Mary Anne solicitously making sure beforehand that he had a thorough medical check-up. Disraeli, who was something of a hypochondriac, was delighted by the result. After that she went with him everywhere, including his family's house at Bradenham, a comfortable, homely place with a quiet scholarly atmosphere. That is, until Mary Anne arrived. Then she would invent parlour games and riddles or try to outwit Disraeli's father with her repertoire of conjuring tricks. Gentle, half-blind, old Isaac liked nothing better than to hear her chatter, while Disraeli's lonely spinster sister longed for her cheerful visits. Mary Anne would walk through the beech woods with Sarah, regaling her with the latest London gossip, or sing ballads for her at the piano, before calling for 'a glass of brandy and water, good and strong'. In an age when for women, only one glass of wine was permissible, Mary Anne showed a healthy liking for alcohol. Before her, Lady Palmerston had on occasions shocked society by refusing to leave the dining-room to the men.

By the time of the 1841 election, Mary Anne was still hard on Disraeli's heels. If Lady Palmerston campaigned for her husband at Tiverton, Mary Anne was indefatigable at Shrewsbury, knocking on doors and bustling into shops at such a rate that a year later the local people still said to Disraeli: 'Such a gay lady, sir! You never can have a dull moment, sir!' The stories of her devotion are countless. Once when they were on their way to the House in a carriage, Mary Anne crushed her hand in the door but endured the pain in silence so as not to upset Disraeli before his speech. Disraeli's tribute to her, when he discovered, was to remove the door and mount it on the wall. Another time when they were dining at Hatfield, Mary Anne asked to be placed at the other end of the table from her husband because she had cut her face on the journey and did not want Disraeli to notice.

She kept every bit of paper he wrote on, even the most cursory and insignificant jottings. In the evenings she spent hours checking manuscripts and making corrections to printers' proofs. Having no children of her own, she came to look on his books as her 'children'. She once wrote in a letter to Lady de Rothschild, 'The first proofs of "Tancred" are now on the table. How much I wish you may be here with me when he is presented to the public, for I am sure you will sympathise with me on my child's fate. What an anxious time for poor me.' Disraeli, for his part, found his concentration helped by her presence. When they were apart, she sent him encouraging little notes on violet-scented paper. 'The more we are separated,' he wrote, 'The more I cling to you . . . unless I had that stimulus I don't think I could go on.' No wonder that when he came to write the dedication in *Sybil*, it was 'to one whose sweet voice has often encouraged, and whose taste and judgement have ever guided its pages; the most severe of critics but – a perfect Wife'.

In the 1841 election, the Conservatives were returned under Sir Robert Peel. Disraeli waited expectantly to be asked to join the Cabinet but no word came from Downing Street. After a week in which he had seen all his less gifted but more orthodox colleagues given ministries, he wrote in desperation to Peel. Mary Anne also did so, although without her husband's knowledge. She had the advantage of being a close friend of Peel's sister but even so, she begged him not to be angry with her for intruding. She was, she said, 'Overwhelmed with anxiety. My husband's political career is for ever crushed, if you do not appreciate him.' He had abandoned literature for politics. 'Do not destroy all his hopes and make him feel his life has been a mistake.' So much for feminine meekness, but Mary Anne also had a practical side. She pointed out firmly to Peel that Disraeli had stood 'four most expensive elections since 1834 . . . and I pledge myself as far as one seat, that it shall always be at your command'. With regard to her own 'humble but enthusiastic exertions for the party . . . they will tell you at Maidstone that more than £40,000 was spent through my influence only'.

Mary Anne put her case as well as she knew how, but Peel, pressured by his party against 'that adventurer', sent back a cool reply. It was Mary Anne, with her sympathy and affection, who helped Disraeli through the next difficult weeks, when to his credit he was patient and loyal to the government. Such disappointment before his marriage would have left him unable to cope. Now he wrote, 'I am tolerably serene, very indeed, when in the company of my guardian angel.' Mary Anne had shown that as well as being a fun-loving 'rattle' she could be single-minded over his career. It was something he would never forget.

But by the winter of 1842 Disraeli had had enough. With Mary Anne he went to Paris to lose his disappointment in a whirl of social gaiety. They dined out eleven nights in succession, once with the Emperor at the Tuileries and met many famous Frenchmen including Dumas and Alfred de Vigny. Not surprisingly, after another visit to Europe in 1845, Mary Anne was 'as . . .

plump as a partridge'. This time they both revelled in the solitude. 'We do not know and have not interchanged a word with a single person of even average intelligence . . . the names of the Duke of Wellington and Sir Robert Peel . . . are quite unknown here.'

If the Disraelis were not moving upwards in politics, they were certainly moving up socially. They now stayed at the best houses in the country and in 1848 acquired a country house and estate of their own. Hughenden Manor in Buckinghamshire was bought with the help of the Bentinck family, Disraeli's strong supporters in the Tory party. It was a seventeenth-century red-brick house, set among beech woods with a view of the Chilterns. Mary Anne, thrilled at being the 'Lady of Hughenden', set about redecorating enthusiastically. In the house she was notoriously unsuccessful, ending up with a hideous mixture of Tudor panelling, Gothic arches and Moorish fretwork. The crimson and yellow Aubusson carpets came from Maples, while shields bought in High Wycombe made the hall look baronial. But the garden she improved greatly, carving out foot paths, laying flower-beds and planting trees. Every day she went to work, dressed in tough boots, a short skirt and gaiters and carrying 'a little lunch and some bottles of beer for the workmen'. She fed the swans called Hero and Leander and Disraeli insisted they also had peacocks on the terrace. He was happiest playing at being the country gentleman and they spent as much time at Hughenden as possible. They went there in the summer after parliament ended and sometimes stayed till Christmas. Disraeli would pace the terrace deep in thought, among the pink geraniums and Grecian statues. In the evenings he strolled through the woods with Mary Anne chattering away beside him in her pony cart. When guests came, he would proudly show them 'the Sylvan scene'. 'My darling, you have . . . done at Hughenden what no other woman, or man either, could do.'

They were seldom without visitors. The Rothschilds, the Prince and Princess of Teck, the Salisburys . . . Disraeli said it was 'as hard work as having a playhouse or keeping an inn'. But Mary Anne always coped efficiently. She was proud of her housekeeping and constantly on the look-out for new ideas. One of her most closely guarded secrets was a recipe for Spanish Pudding learnt on her honeymoon. The local shopkeepers found her too economical and told stories about the time she sent back a quarter of cheese because Disraeli would not be there to eat it. If she was ever ill, Disraeli was lost without her organization. 'Complete anarchy', he called it to a friend.

Their visits to other houses were less successful. Disraeli disliked hunting and shooting. 'Whenever we go to a country house,' wrote Mary Anne, '. . . Dizzy is not only bored, and has constant ennui, but he takes to eating as a resource; he eats at breakfast, luncheon and dinner; the result is . . . he becomes dreadfully bilious, and we have to come away.' Meanwhile, Mary Anne's own oddities were at their most noticeable in an aristocratic drawing-room. At one house she scolded her hostess, 'I find your house is packed with improper pictures. There's a horrible one in our room. Dizzy says it is Venus and Adonis. I had to stay awake half the night to keep him from looking at it.' Another time they stayed in a house where Lord Hardinge had the bedroom next to them. Mary Anne greeted him ecstatically at breakfast: 'How lucky I am! I've been sleeping between the greatest orator and the greatest soldier of the day.' During a discussion among some ladies about Grecian statues, she interrupted with, 'Oh, but you ought to see my Dizzy in his bath.'

There was also her bizarre appearance, always a fantastic jumble of feathers, lace and bows. Most women took to caps and shawls at forty, but at sixty Mary Anne could be seen skipping in her garden in a white muslin dress and a straw hat with velvet ribbons. A *Book of Beauty* published in 1841 described her as 'a very fairy'. When she was eighty and the fashion was tight lacing, she would appear in a shapeless, red velvet tunic, her wig slightly awry and a huge miniature of Disraeli pinned to her chest like a decoration.

When people became used to her eccentricity, many of them came to like her. As Lady Battersea said, 'One could smile at her absurdities and love her all the same . . . if foolish and at times even ridiculous, she was a splendid wife.' Even Sir Stafford Northcote meeting her for the first time, found 'something very warm and good in her manner which makes one forgive a few oddities'. With those who were less generous, Disraeli was always there to protect her with what an onlooker described as his 'gracious, half protective, half deferential attitude'. He had never forgotten that 'she believed in me when men despised me' or as Lady Battersea put it, 'Mr Disraeli knew what he owed her, and she never doubted this.' And so he would not allow anyone to show the slightest disrespect towards her and once left the house of a party leader who had mocked Mary Anne. To someone who asked him why he did it, he replied in one word, 'Gratitude'.

But life was not all socializing. Disraeli worked hard to progress in his career. The debates in 1846 over the Corn Bill often lasted till 4 or 5 a.m. No matter how late he returned Mary Anne was always up to welcome him with a burning fire and blazing lights. She sometimes went down to the House in a carriage and waited for him with a cold supper ready.

By 1851 Disraeli's hopes had been dashed rather too frequently. He was, Mary Anne observed anxiously, 'very much *down*'. To cheer him they attended the

Great Exhibition in the Crystal Palace, that 'enchanted pile'. Mary Anne sat at the top table for luncheon along with Catherine Gladstone and Lady John Russell. With typical tactlessness she interrupted Lady John as she tried to make her young son eat. 'Ah, the child has too much soul to be hungry, don't trouble him to eat.' Possibly, she was nervous. She was still despised by much of society, which took its lead from Queen Victoria who thought her 'very vulgar'. Certainly, Lady John favoured the Gladstones socially as well as politically. Disraeli had been considered 'too theatrical' ever since he arrived to dinner in a 'bright rose-coloured shirt-front'. Nevertheless Disraeli's time was coming. 1851 was the year of Palmerston's dismissal and 1852 saw Russell's fall. In the Tory administration that followed, Disraeli was asked to join Lord Derby's Cabinet. A proud but delighted Mary Anne wrote a letter of congratulation to 'The Right Honourable the Chancellor of the Exchequer'.

Now began what Disraeli called 'the glittering bustle'. Mary Anne went to her first Court Drawing-Room, covered in lace and diamonds as usual. Although dressed in all her finery, she thought only of Disraeli beside her and was convinced that the Queen noticed him more than anyone else. 'My heart, dear Sa, was full of gratified ambition.' In 1861, a coveted invitation came to stay at Windsor. Mary Anne, in a frenzy of excitement, remembered every detail to write to Sarah and old Mr Disraeli at Bradenham. She was rather shocked that the Queen of England slept 'without pillows or bolster' and 'had no second convenience'. The greatest honour came in 1863 with the wedding of the Prince of Wales to Princess Alexandra of Denmark. Disraeli noted gleefully that he had been invited 'and what is still more marked Mrs D too' while many 'great ladies had not'.

He was always quick to share every triumph with

Mary Anne. On the evening in 1867 that saw the passing of the Reform Bill, he was overwhelmed with invitations to supper from his enthusiastic supporters. But he knew that Mary Anne would be waiting and sure enough she was – with a pie from Fortnum and Mason's and a bottle of champagne. It was then that he paid her his famous compliment, 'Why, my dear, you are more like a mistress than a wife.' She was now in her seventies. Later that year they went to Scotland where Disraeli was given the freedom of the City of Edinburgh. 'We were so delighted with our reception, Mrs Disraeli and I, that we danced a jig in our bedroom.' But by now, as one observant onlooker noticed, Mary Anne was battling with illness. He thought she looked 'like a witch in Macbeth' and her husband like a wizard 'with his olive complexion and coal black eyes'.

In 1868 she collapsed and had to take to her bed for some weeks. Gladstone, who often had tea with Mary Anne and was very fond of her, asked after her health in the House. In his reply Disraeli said, 'My wife has always had a strong regard for you . . . being of a vivid and original character, she can comprehend and value your great gifts and qualities.' If it was true, she was being more charitable than Catherine Gladstone ever was to Disraeli. Shortly afterwards Disraeli also fell ill, with gout. They communicated by letter from their bedrooms and, typically, Mary Anne kept all his letters to her, tied up carefully in a packet and labelled 'Notes from dear Dizzy during our illness when we could not leave our rooms'. One of them read, 'Grosvenor Gate has become a hospital but a hospital with you is worth a palace with anybody else. Your own D.' Another thanked her for 'the most amusing and charming letter I ever had. It beats Horace Walpole and Mme de Sévigné.' This time they both recovered but for Mary Anne it was the beginning of the end, the first outbreak of the cancer from which she would die in five years' time.

But there was one supreme triumph yet to come, the triumph they had all along been working for. In February 1868 Lord Derby resigned and Disraeli became Prime Minister. They had a great celebration at the Foreign Office because Mary Anne thought Downing Street 'so dingy and decaying'. The guests included the Prince and Princess of Wales and anyone of importance in the country. One of them remembers seeing 'Dizzy in his glory leading about the Prince of Wales', but it was already too late for Mrs Dizzy, she followed behind 'looking very ill and haggard'.

He was not to stay Prime Minister for long. Ten months later there was a Liberal victory. He knew he might not be in power again and if he was, Mary Anne would probably not live to see it. So just before he resigned, Disraeli made her a gesture of love and gratitude. He did not want a peerage for himself, preferring to stay in the Lower House, but asked that the honour be granted to his wife 'which perhaps under ordinary circumstances Your Majesty would have deigned to bestow on him'. So Mary Anne became Viscountess Beaconsfield. If the Queen had her doubts she did not show it, and although some people must have laughed, others did not grudge her her obvious delight. Within a week she was using coroneted writing paper and embroidering B's all over her furniture and book-covers.

By this time she knew she had cancer of the stomach but tried to hide it from Disraeli, little knowing he was doing the same. She still struggled to go out in society, although she could not eat and was frequently racked with pain. In 1872 the French chargé d'affaires saw her at a party looking like some strange Eastern potentate in her jewels and velvet, her shrunken face still brightly painted. She also insisted on going to Manchester where Disraeli was to speak at a great Conservative rally.

Afterwards, in the tumultuous applause, she forgot her age and illness and ran to meet him, exclaiming excitedly, 'Oh, Dizzy, Dizzy, it is the greatest night of all. This pays for all.'

But the effort had exhausted her. She was seriously ill on returning to London although she still went out occasionally to parties. She was completely accepted now in society and known to everyone simply as Mary Anne. In the country they still called her 'Mrs Dizzy' as it 'has become a household word'. On 9 May 1872 she collapsed at a court reception and went down to recover at Hughenden. But she struggled back for the rest of the season until in July she had to leave another party, smiling and chattering away as usual to hide her great pain. Shortly afterwards at a second palace reception, she was so ill, she had to be smuggled out. After that she stayed at home. She was too ill even to go to Hughenden. A heartbroken Disraeli stayed with her in London for the summer and took her for long drives through the suburbs to keep her mind off the pain. He wrote miserably to friends, 'To see her every day weaker and weaker is heartrending; to witness the gradual death of one who has shared so long and so completely my life entirely unmans me.' And he added, 'We have been married for thirty years and I have never been bored with her.' And Mary Anne as death drew nearer, worried about leaving him. Once when he had leant on a pedestal to be photographed, Mary Anne had rushed to remove it. 'Dizzy has never had anyone but me to lean on, and he shan't be shown with a prop now.' Between themselves, he was her 'eagle' while she was his 'little dove'. It could well have been the other way round.

In September she rallied and they went together to their beloved Hughenden. At first she could move about the grounds in a wheelchair but she soon grew too weak even for that and would sit at her window watching the peacocks on the terrace. She missed especially her visits to the village where the local children adored her. Childless herself, she would pick them up and hug them, quite forgetting that she was meant to act the lady of the manor. She still insisted on receiving guests so that Disraeli would have some cheerful company. In November she had a house-party for some old friends. They found her 'sadly altered in looks since London – death written in her face – but as usual gorgeously dressed'.

This was the last glimpse society had of her. In December she caught pneumonia and suffered from congestion of the lung. Disraeli who was 'totally unable to meet the catastrophe' did not leave her room for a week and left his secretary to answer the Queen's enquiries. She would not go to bed. Her last drink was a draught of her favourite ale. She died in her chair like Queen Elizabeth after days of hallucinations when she had even turned against Disraeli.

But it was only madness caused by her illness. After her death Disraeli found among her papers hundreds of small, sealed packets containing locks of his hair. For 33 years Mary Anne had cut and dyed his black ringlets and she could not bring herself to throw them away. In another envelope with a tiny ring, was a note in her careful writing: 'Dizzy's wedding-ring, taken off today because my hand and finger is swollen. July 6th 1872.' Finally, there was a letter, written before she died, urging him to remarry and be happy. 'Do not live alone dearest. Someone I earnestly hope you may find as attached to you as your own devoted Mary Anne.' Disraeli's forlorn reply was, 'She was the most cheerful and courageous woman I knew.'

She was buried at Hughenden Church on a windy, wet winter's day. Disraeli stood bare-headed for several minutes in the pouring rain gazing bleakly down at her coffin. Meanwhile letters of condolence poured in –

from the Queen, Prime Minister Gladstone and countless others. Gladstone recalled his own happy marriage in the same year as Disraeli's. 'It has been permitted to both of us to enjoy a priceless boon through a third of a century. Spared myself the blow which has fallen on you, I can form some conception of what it must have been and be.' Just how lonely he was, Disraeli revealed in his own letter a year later to Lord John Russell: 'In your retirement you have the inestimable happiness of constant and accomplished sympathy, without which life is little worth. Mine is lone and dark . . .'

Shortly after her marriage to Disraeli, Mary Anne had drawn up a list of his and her characteristics. Under him she had written, 'He is a genius' and under herself, 'She is a dunce . . . she is not to be depended on . . . she has no ambition and hates politics.' In fact, she was not doing herself justice. She was recognized, as no other politician's wife ever had been, as the stable factor behind Disraeli's genius. And proof of this lies in *The Times*'s obituary on 16 December 1872: 'Who would have supposed 35 years ago, that the coming history of English political life would take a direction from the unselfish affection of a woman, and a woman not marked by any unusual capacities? Society would have been as little likely to single out the widow of Mr Wyndham Lewis as destined to play an important part in life as the politicians of the day would have been inclined to see in Mr Disraeli the future leader of the Tory party. Yet the marriage which sprang from that affection was an historical event.'

Mrs Gladstone

William and Catherine Gladstone were born within twenty miles of each other but in very different circumstances. Catherine was the adored, indulged elder daughter of an historic Whig family, the aristocratic Glynnes, who could claim descent from four former Prime Ministers and trace their line back beyond the Norman Conquest. It was a long way from their splendid seat at Hawarden, standing sentinel over the foothills of the Welsh mountains, to the solid brick house in Liverpool where the Gladstones lived the lives of typical, newly-rich merchants. Not until a son of the house, William, worked his way upwards by sheer brains and industry was there much likelihood that socially the two would ever meet.

Catherine, or 'Pussy' as she was nicknamed, grew up in the privileged world of the landowning rich. Only a few months of the year were spent at Hawarden, the rest with a string of distinguished relations. Most often the Glynne children stayed with Grandpapa, Lord Braybrooke, at Audley End but also at great houses like Escrick or Vale Royal and with a beloved elderly aunt, 'dear Chat', who was Lady Chatham, Hester Chatham's daughter-in-law.

It was an active, outdoor life and they excelled at archery and riding. Catherine was never highly educated, though she could speak French and Italian fluently and quote reams of poetry by heart, and for all her adult life she was seldom seen with a book in her hand. As a child she was a tomboy, rumbustiously healthy, with a mass of blonde curls. She despised routine, thrived on adventure, and even then lived life to the full. Impulsive and loving, especially towards her mother and her younger sister Mary whom she led into all sorts of childish scrapes, she was also known for her fearful temper. 'Pussy's passions', they were called in the nursery.

The two sisters, Catherine and Mary, were launched upon London society in 1830 after a winter in Paris when they were presented to the French Royal Family. The whole of that then-exclusive London world was open to them. They went to theatres, operas, Almack's, to a fancy-dress ball dressed as Night and Dawn and later, to Queen Victoria's coronation where they had seats reserved for them in the Abbey. Catherine was by now tall and slender with perfect colouring and wide-set blue eyes. Her sister was less flamboyant but more delicate and between them they had no shortage of suitors. They had also no intention of getting married, being devoted to each other and to family life at Hawarden. In fact Catherine was 27 when she married, a year off what Jane Austen described as middle-aged.

By this time her mother was debilitated by a stroke and Catherine, as Gladstone noted shrewdly in his diary, reigned at Hawarden like a queen, carrying everything by her vitality and exuberance, her mother, brothers and sisters clustering round her 'like planets round a sun'.

She may have met Gladstone as early as 1831 when she visited her brother Henry at Oxford. A friend of Gladstone's, Robert Phillimore, shared rooms with Henry at Christ Church. But if she did, he did not sufficiently impress her to stop her falling in love with another man.

We do not know much about Colonel Francis Harcourt except that he was a connection of the Archbishop of York and equerry to the Duchess of Kent. In 1837 he jilted the 25 year-old Catherine for an earl's daughter, Lady Charlotte Jenkinson. The betrayal seems to have affected Catherine deeply and her solicitous family swept her off to Europe to recover. At Ems in autumn 1838 they met a rising young Tory politician, the gifted, handsome MP for Newark. William Gladstone had been ordered abroad by his doctors, suffering from overwork and grief over the death of his mother. He was travelling with his invalid sister and Catherine, noting the meeting in her journal, was 'much struck by his pretty attentions to Miss Gladstone who is an invalid'. About William himself she does not say much, except that he was rather too 'matter-of-fact'. But this was only a first impression. A month or so later she was to come to know him better. They found themselves in the same hotel in Naples and from then onwards her diary is full of him. 'Mr Gladstone dined with us, a very agreeable evening . . . To the church of San Ferdinando with Mr Gladstone and heard a most extraordinary sermon.' They dined together, lunched together, visited the museum and climbed Vesuvius. By the time the Glynne party left for Rome in December they knew him well enough to tease him with the nickname 'Gia'. It must have been quite a revelation to the over-earnest young man who once scolded someone for buying apples on a Sunday and in all seriousness thought up thirty-nine reasons why a religious person could go to parties. No wonder he was fascinated by Catherine's carefree, affectionate nature, her ready laughter and quick, graceful movements. And Catherine with all the assurance of her background was not in the least over-awed by the brilliant young politician who, people were already saying, would be Prime Minister one day. On the contrary, she showed him how to relax, made him laugh at himself and at life and brought out a side of his nature which many had doubted was there.

Next day William followed the Glynnes to Rome and there it was his turn to make the discovery – that Catherine was not all girlish frivolity. She had great charity and no personal vanity. She never spent money on herself. One day in the church of Santa Maria Maggiore, the two of them discussed this question and Catherine turned to William to ask earnestly, 'Do you think that we can possibly be justified in indulging ourselves in so much luxury?' That same night he confided to his diary, 'I loved her for that question.'

The problem was how to tell her. He was tormented by feelings of unworthiness. The first time he tried to propose he had all the trappings of the moonlit Colosseum but he found himself tongue-tied with nervousness. Catherine made no move to help, though she regretted it later when telling her children. A fortnight later he tried again by letter. The result was pompous and stilted. The worst sentence had 141 words! But William was lucky in that Catherine could see beyond his dreadful earnestness. Her reaction was to play for time so that when William left for England he may not have been accepted but he had not been refused. One of their last meetings was at Porta Maggiore, supposedly to inspect a newly-discovered Roman tomb. Catherine's diary shows that her thoughts were elsewhere. 'The bas-reliefs are in good preservation, they depict the – ' she says and does not finish. By now it must have been easy for anyone but William to see what her true feelings were. She sent messages to him through her brother and copied out extracts from his book, *State and Church*, a labour of love if anything was.

When the Glynnes arrived home in April 1839, William became a frequent visitor to their house in Berkeley Square. Here he had the encouragement and support of her family. Even her brother Stephen, now head of the family, wrote to ask him his intentions. 'There is no one to whom I would so gladly entrust my sister as to you, feeling convinced that there is no one who would be so worthy of such a prize.' It says a lot for William's political prospects that this could be said to the fourth son of a Liverpool merchant. On 8 June 1839 the couple attended a garden party in Fulham. They took a quiet walk by the river and, wrote Gladstone, 'here my Catherine gave me herself'. He added, 'She asked for the earliest Communion that we might go together to the Altar of Christ.'

The two sisters always did things together. Nine days later Mary accepted Lord Lyttelton. On 25 July 1839, Hawarden's bells rang for a double wedding with both brides dressed alike in white satin and the church, as the local paper put it, 'crammed to suffocation with females'. The only absentee was their mother who was so overcome at the occasion that she insisted on remaining behind at the house, deserted even by her own maid. The Gladstones honeymooned at Norton Priory, Cheshire, the seat of Sir Richard Brooke, whose daughter, Harriet, was a close friend of Catherine's.

In fact, Harriet's teasing comment on hearing of Catherine's engagement was that now she was to marry a methodical man, perhaps he would teach her to answer her letters. Catherine never managed an orderly correspondence but if she changed William, he also changed her. By nature she was untidy, unpunctual and forgetful yet she schooled herself never to keep William waiting and to write careful household accounts. The kitchen staff were trained to have a hot meal waiting, no matter what time William returned from the Commons.

A part of her rebelled at the change. She would say to him, 'What a bore you would have been if you had married someone as tidy as yourself.' She was impatient also of his longwindedness and dismissed his beloved political arguments as so much 'red tape'. Like her sister Mary she found it difficult to accept a husband who spent every spare moment reading, even when waiting for a train. But these were small complaints. The important thing as far as Catherine was concerned was that at last she had found someone stronger than herself. In many of her letters she calls him her 'dear old oak' while she is the clinging ivy. From someone as spirited and strong-willed as Catherine this was praise indeed.

The newly married couple moved into a house in Carlton House Terrace in London. William helped Catherine furnish it. 'Beauty is beauty even in furniture.' Together they chose china and pictures and a setting for his fine collection of ivories. One of the first things they did was to set up a servants' library. They entertained with musical soirées and began the famous Thursday 10 a.m. breakfasts. William was always at his best at breakfast and this remained a fixture of their lives.

In 1841 when the Tories took office William became Vice-President of the Board of Trade and Peel's main ally in fiscal reform. Now pressures of work often kept him away from Catherine. 'It is a little dreary,' she wrote in her diary. And to her sister: 'Oh dear it is mournful work. Here am I and him gone off at eight o'clock, just having swallowed his dinner. I now seldom get any sort of talk and even at breakfast he is reading the newspaper.' She worried about his health. He was now working a fourteen-hour day. 'I wish he would have a horse; one ride a week would be better than nothing.' But she was soon to be occupied with her children. Willy had been born in June 1840 and Agnes followed in 1842. Between 1842 and 1854 she was to have a further six children, three boys and three girls, whom she nursed herself against the fashion of the time. She was an ever-present figure in the nursery, supervising the nannies, noting down any signs of progress and administering the countless pills and potions with which she also plied her husband. In 1845 when Gladstone resigned from the Board of Trade she took Willy to see his father's office. 'He read the words "Board of Trade" on the door, and I made him look well at the room and at what he calls Papa being at his lessons, for I should wish him to remember visiting him hereafter.'

The first big problem they were to come up against concerned the Glynne family finances at Hawarden. Stephen was more interested in church architecture than estate management and left matters with a dissolute, dishonest agent. As a result the whole estate went downhill until by 1847 it was bankrupt. Stephen fled abroad and to Catherine's pride, the whole family turned to William. She was convinced that his 'good old head and his wits' alone could save it. William's was all the hard work and worry but Catherine backed him up with stringent economy. Her clothes had always been home-made and her favourite ornament a fresh flower pinned to her bodice. Her foreign maid complained despairingly, 'We had no time, Mrs Gladstone just *yumped* into her clothes.' Now she borrowed what she could from her sister and thought twice about a second-class rail fare. '1/– sandwiches, 3d. milk for baby, 1/3 for two cups of tea, in all 3/– with bun and biscuit.' And as usual she started organizing Mary. Did she really need a second laundry maid and how much beer was drunk in the servants' hall?

To both William and Catherine it was worth it so long as they could keep their beloved Hawarden. To Catherine this was still home and William had come to love it just as much. With no country house of their own, eventually they arranged to share Hawarden with Stephen who was only too glad to have the responsibility taken from him. With characteristically impulsive generosity,

Catherine opened the park. 'To me it is quite horrid, the entire solitude and the feeling that scarcely anybody may enjoy the innocent pleasures of the lovely park.'

From here Catherine wrote many of her thousands of letters, mostly to William in London. While his letters to her were neatly headed and accurately dated, hers to him were a breathless, illegible scrawl, unsigned, misspelt, unpunctuated and spattered with smudges and blots. She would write on any scrap of paper, even round the edges of old letters. She once wrote to her daughter on egg-sandwich wrappings in a train. Yet every sentence pulsates with life and her own racy, highly individual sense of style, a legacy from the Glynnes who had always talked an esoteric family slang. In 1851 Lord Lyttelton compiled the privately printed *Glynnese Glossary*; 'the chief authorities are Mrs Gladstone and Lady Lyttelton, principally the former.' Much of this private language reflected Catherine's impatience with anything slow. She had a way of expressing herself that went straight to the point. 'Really he is A2'; 'his life is lived on a pinnacle'; 'vull' instead of 'null and void'. Some of our current day expressions like 'over the moon' and 'to die of laughter' have their origins in Glynne family slang.

To her husband in particular her letters were a hotch-potch of gossip, politics and domestic problems. When William was deeply involved in the Free Trade question, he still found time to deal with a bad-tempered governess; when he became Leader of the House, he still went shopping for sponges and china. It was Morley who pointed out that Gladstone did not go home for peace. He may have gone for harmony and reassurance but his recreation from work was yet more work. He might be destined to be leader of the nation but at home he remained very much head of the family.

Apart from her letters to her husband, Catherine wrote every day to her sister, Mary. They still remained as close and exchanged constant visits. Vast pilgrimages of mothers, nannies and babies would set out from Hawarden to the great Lyttelton mansion at Hagley. Catherine's diary is full of 'Left Hawarden, seventeen of us without counting the children' or 'Lytteltons went away, eighteen souls in all'. There were also visits to the royal nursery where the Dowager Lady Lyttleton was a governess. The Queen had married within six months of Catherine and her children were much the same age.

But in 1850 Catherine's daughter Jessy died of meningitis. She had suffered terribly during her short illness, so to that extent Catherine was relieved for her. At any rate it was she who preserved her equanimity when William had collapsed with grief. Such was his agony that the family began to fear for him also. Typically, William's way of assuaging his grief was to write a long memoir, including details of Jessy's illness and its symptoms. Catherine's epitaph was simpler but more human. 'She was a darling baby.'

As if this blow was not enough she next lost her sister-in-law, Henry's wife, Lavinia, who died giving birth to her fourth daughter, leaving a distraught husband and bewildered children. Catherine, who could not bear to see others in distress, was ordered to rest abroad by her doctors. In Naples, preoccupied, exhausted and disconsolate, she suffered a miscarriage in November 1850. In fact, for once her general ill-health kept her from sharing in the life of her husband. In Naples he visited political prisoners, suffering intense revulsion at the conditions in which they were held. It was this which set him on the long journey towards Liberalism, and the excitement finally restored Catherine's spirits.

She was always eager to see him in the centre of the political arena, and was never happier than when she heard him speak. Visitors to the Ladies' Gallery in the

House of Commons would be shown a certain patch of brass railing, polished till it shone by the clutch of Mrs Gladstone's gloved hand. During the famous debate on the Corn Laws, she sat next to Lady John Russell. She regarded William's health as a sacred trust and herself made the celebrated egg-nog he sipped in the House to soothe his throat. Sometimes in the thick of a crowd of supporters when he began to tire of shaking hands, she would slip unnoticed behind him and proffer her hand instead of his.

Yet in spite of everything, she was not a good politician's wife. She was not interested in drawing-room politics and so missed many opportunities to coax a straying sheep back to the party fold, or, more important, to soothe those others whom William had unwittingly affronted by shortsightedly ignoring them in the House. Anyone in the least dull bored her immediately. She chose her guests for sensational rather than politically profitable results. Calls were not returned, invitations were sent out late or not at all – some were once discovered down the back of the drawing-room sofa – and on more than one occasion when the guests arrived, she had forgotten to change. To be fair to Catherine, she did not mean to be deliberately rude, but like William she often seemed to be in another world. If anything she was the more acute but they both had their own very definite set of values and tended to assume that everyone strove for their ideals. There was a famous instance when they tried to engage a cook. Catherine wrote quite innocently in her diary, 'Engaged a cook after a long conversation about religious matters, chiefly between her and William. She interested me greatly.'

There were also her charitable duties which took up more and more of her time. In the 1850s, after Jessy's death, William began his rescue work among the London prostitutes. Catherine joined in too. 'Yesterday,' she wrote, 'I took a poor young thing to the new House, picked her up in Windmill Street and left her safe.' While William tracked the girls down in the backstreets, Catherine founded shelters, raised funds and sat on committees. In an age when most well-born ladies never even mentioned the word 'prostitute', Gladstone could reply to someone who asked, 'What will your wife say if you bring this woman home with you?', 'Why, it is to my wife that I am taking her.' So much seems undeniable and yet the fact is palpable from Gladstone's diaries that his rescue work was much more concentrated when Catherine was out of London. Possibly at a time when so many subscribed to the strict Augustinian doctrine (i.e. that sex, even between married couples, was sinful unless for procreation), there was an element of substitution in his crusade. But the integrity of his actions cannot be questioned, although inevitably among his contemporaries who did not know him well, there were rumours.

If she heard them, Catherine was totally untouched by them. In any case she had the feeling that whatever William did was guided by God. Unlike her husband she did not talk about religion much. She simply took it as a fact of life that a special Being watched over his career. In 1854 she wrote to a friend, 'We have been signally guarded and protected . . . I . . . feel that a special Providence has guarded him and that truth has prevailed so far in the long run. I must not forget that a reverse may come, only most certainly it would not be for me to be a little trustful from experience alone.'

It seemed as if her confidence was justified when in 1853 Gladstone became Chancellor of the Exchequer in Lord Aberdeen's government. Shortly before, he had made a brilliant speech against Disraeli's budget. Catherine, who was travelling, had rushed to 'claw' a copy of *The Times*. 'Oh, that I could have been with you there and afterwards.' All her life she loved to be at the centre of things. She could, she said, endure a life that was tragic but never one that was humdrum. During the Crimean War she wrote wistfully from Hawarden, 'It feels very odd here, so quiet, I don't think I like it for in London one could feel to be of some use in the war troubles, whilst it seems unnatural to hear the twaddle remarks and croaking of country friends with no reliable information and no hope of details.' Nevertheless, Catherine was among the few women involved in the war effort. She knitted countless mufflers and sent Fortnum and Mason parcels to the trenches of Sebastopol.

In 1855 Aberdeen resigned and Gladstone took office briefly under Lord Palmerston. Catherine disliked 'the violent Pam' as she disliked most of William's colleagues. In her heart she probably suspected them of stealing her husband's thunder. Just as she had inveighed against Peel when Gladstone served under him, now she castigated the Liberal leaders especially 'the shuffling John Russell . . . the clog which will one day drag you . . . down'.

Certainly, Lord John had his blind spots but Gladstone was not one of them. He liked his younger colleague and did his best to help him. Lady John too, was friendly. The four met frequently at country houses like Drumlanrig. Often the Gladstones were asked to dine or to tea at Pembroke Lodge on summer Sundays. Lord John and Gladstone would pace the garden, discussing natural history, a mutual interest. Lady John adored Gladstone and wrote warmly to Catherine about his many triumphs. William and Catherine were among the chosen few admitted to see Lord John before he died. However, Catherine remained suspicious. No one could measure up to William. She would have preferred him to stand alone with 'a nice party assembled round you, surely many, many would joyfully follow you!'

But for the present she could daydream about the day he became Prime Minister. Within the family she sent out half-joking invitations: 'Lord and Lady Lyttelton and Mrs Gladstone request the honour of the Prime Minister's company at dinner on Saturday and Sunday.' Meanwhile, she was comforted by the thought that 'whatever William decides will be right . . . To doubt William's sense and judgement seems altogether extraordinary.' All the same she was glad when he resigned although she could admit in private to Mary, 'After all the excitement of feeling how grand our speeches were, how fine and bold the line which William had taken, the reality and bother of packing up comes upon one . . .'

She was not going to be able to confide in Mary much longer. After eleven children, Mary's doctors had warned her against another, but by the autumn of 1856 a twelfth child was expected. Catherine had to cope with the nursing as well as running the great house at Hagley where the nurse had collapsed and the cook had suspected smallpox. For once the relief at the birth in February 1857 was too much even for her composure. She rushed into the Hagley schoolroom for 'a quiet cry' with her nieces. But by July Mary was so weak that she took to her bed permanently, and Catherine, who knew it was hopeless, had to bear the tragedy without the one person who could give her support. William was heavily committed in parliament and could not be spared from the House. She wrote gallant letters to him: 'I should not wish you to leave your duty, that would do me no good' – but occasionally it was all too much for her. 'And yet I do feel at moments that my heart would break when I look at her.'

Ironically, the two sisters drew even closer together as Mary's life ebbed out of her. She clung for strength to Catherine, 'so warm, so life-giving', until on 17 August 1857, she died in Catherine's arms. Apart from losing

William, no greater blow could have befallen Catherine. Losing her precious sister was a turning-point in her life. After this she faced middle age without the same carefree vitality.

As usual her way out of her grief was to comfort others. There were the twelve Lyttelton children whom she adopted and loved as her own. Later, when her brother-in-law, John Gladstone, died she mothered his orphaned family too. She was constantly being called in to nurse an invalid or take some child to convalesce by the seaside. She even found time to worry about the Queen and wrote to William anxiously, 'I devour your letters eagerly and am shocked about the weight, I wish H.M. would seriously consider Banting, really her age is nothing and what may not her size become eight or ten years hence?' Unemployed men were given work building roads at Hawarden and children from the Lancashire cotton famine given shelter. At one time, during the famine, Catherine is said to have provided over a thousand meals a day. In 1866 a great cholera epidemic swept through London's East End killing 8000 people. Catherine toiled fearlessly and tirelessly in the hospitals, where the staff had fled for fear of infection, and took sick children into her home. When the worst of the illness was over she led the struggle for convalescent homes, writing persistent letters to *The Times* begging for money. A few orphans were housed at Hawarden where Catherine visited them and played with them frequently. As soon as she appeared at the door she would be buried in an avalanche of excited children. Then she would open her bag and distribute titbits saved from her dinner parties.

With all this mountain of work, she still went religiously to the Commons, rushing from the East End, usually by underground or on foot. Even as the Prime Minister's wife she used public transport. 'I find the trams very useful,' one letter read, 'but full this week. Having sprung on one a rough driver nearly pushed me off as the inside was fullissimus.' No wonder her favourite niece, Lucy Lyttelton, suggested it might be too tiring. 'How is she to do it . . . with all her innumerable other kind deeds and her season and societyums and be deep in politics and be everything to Uncle William – all at once? She looks terrible fagged already.' Catherine's reaction was swift: 'I can never take amiss anything you say and I know love prompts it, but I must just observe that the House of Commons is almost my only real relaxation. I don't mean that just the exciting bits may not tire, but on the whole it comforts me. I can look at him and be at peace.'

In fact, for William the early 1860s were a trying time politically. He was now Chancellor of the Exchequer in Palmerston's government, having finally made up his mind to cross the floor of the House and join the Liberals. Many of his old friends were dead but in 1861 Catherine wrote to Sir James Graham, one of the few survivors, asking him to speak on William's budget. 'He does not know I am telling you this . . . Even a few words thrown in by you would refresh William's spirit . . . No one knows but myself what he has gone through in the last two years . . .' She was right of course. William was not as resilient as his great rival Disraeli and took any political blows personally. In his worst moments he would turn to Catherine to confide in. Years ago when they first married he had given her the choice between knowing all his political secrets and keeping silent, or knowing nothing so she need not worry. Naturally she chose the former and from then on, she kept her word. After fifty years of marriage, Gladstone could say with gratitude, 'My wife has known every political secret I have ever had, and has never betrayed my confidence.' But her role was that of a sounding board. He may have confided in her but he did not consult her. Still, she was grateful whenever he turned to her 'to deposit the wonderful anxiety'.

At last her belief in him was rewarded. On 1 December 1868, the Queen's telegram announced him Prime Minister. Significantly, the family did not move to Downing Street. Even as Prime Minister's wife, Catherine did not intend to be a political hostess. Life at Carlton House Terrace remained as informal as ever and an unexpected visitor might still find his hostess dining on the sofa off a single peach. Hawarden was no more organized. Guests were often not met at the station. The future Lord Kilbracken had to trudge two miles through a snowstorm with his luggage in a hawker's cart.

In March 1873 Gladstone's government was defeated in the Commons and he seized the opportunity to tell his family that after the election he would retire. Catherine was adamantly against it, even when the Liberals were defeated. She wrote heatedly in 1874 when Disraeli took office, 'Is it not disgusting after all Papa's labour and patriotism and years of work to think of handing over his nest-egg to that Jew?' In fact, in her blind devotion to her husband she began to lose her sense of proportion. She had always disliked Disraeli but now he was not merely wrong but evil. Once, when arriving at Hawarden she wrote, 'I feel as if out of d'Izzy's atmosphere, and the air is so fresh and sweet.' Within the family William always came first, sometimes to the exclusion of her children. When her daughter Agnes went lame, her first thought was inexcusably selfish, 'Supposing it had been me instead of Agnes, oh, what should we have done.' Quite apart from being simply unkind, such an attitude could not help William. He would have been far better served by discriminating and constructive criticism. But in Catherine's eyes his only fault was what she deemed excessive modesty. 'It may be a *fault* sometimes in great positions . . . I never can make him think himself a great man! Which everyone else thinks, or should think,' she added firmly. To an unimpressed colleague she was living 'too much in the neighbourhood of fools' paradise'.

Her views were reinforced by Gladstone's popularity with the public. 'The people's William', Catherine called him proudly. Thousands flocked to see him at Hawarden which his wife accepted calmly as his due. She liked nothing better than the walk to church through admiring crowds. In 1879 as the Liberal candidate for Midlothian they toured his constituency triumphantly. For her the excitement was so great that she collapsed with an old skin complaint, erysipelas. She recovered in 1880 in time for the election. Three Gladstones were returned in a great triumph for Liberalism and Catherine of course was convinced that only her husband could direct it. She wrote to Lucy more eloquently than honestly, '. . . would it not be cowardly to think of self when the giant's hand is needed? . . . I never looked upon Father but that he was the nation's. I have seen him go forth ill, I have seen him going forth exhausted night after night, leaving home, wife, children. Shall he fail now in his country's cause? The mighty, the brave spirit, if he is wanted shall he shrink now? no.' However, even her daughter later admitted, 'It was he who ached for retirement, she who encouraged him to remain. To her his longing for resignation was frankly a great trial. She made no secret of it. She loved the atmosphere, the stimulus of battle; she was ever eager for the fray, and from her own point of view, she would have longed for him to die in harness.'

So at the age of seventy, William Gladstone was again Prime Minister. He had the ordinary people behind him but society led by the Queen did not share their views. Victoria even neglected to invite him to her son, the Duke of Connaught's wedding. Yet still Catherine refused to admit that anything was wrong. Only once did she strike the right note with William, when she admonished him as he was about to leave for Windsor: 'Now, contrary to your ways, do *pet* the Queen, and for once believe you can, you dear old thing.'

Luckily for the Gladstones there was always Hawarden, which they considered their real home, with its simple and comforting routine. Catherine rose to a cold bath every morning, even in her eighties. She was not interested in comfort and would not have a carpet in her bedroom. 'I adhere to having my floor scrubbed constantly with soap.' Before breakfast she accompanied William a mile uphill to early service, with him throwing sticks for the dog while she looked through the morning post, leaving a trail of discarded letters and envelopes behind her. After breakfast William would work in the Temple of Peace, his library, until the afternoon when he took his favourite exercise of chopping down trees in the park. At 5 p.m. there was tea and reading round the fire – Keble, Scott, *Nicholas Nickleby* – until it was time to dress for dinner. Catherine had very little prudery and often walked around upstairs in nothing but a bath towel. The evenings were often spent in music as many musicians stayed there, including the Swedish singer, Jenny Lind. Whoever came was expected to visit Catherine's two charity homes in Hawarden Park. When all was well at Hawarden, William and Catherine would stand together on the hearth-rug with their arms round each others' waists, swaying happily to the tune of,

'A ragamuffin husband and a rantipoling wife,
We'll fiddle it and scrape it through the ups and downs of life.'

But all was not well. On 6 May 1882 the Gladstones dined at the Austrian Embassy. They returned to the tragic news that Lord Frederick Cavendish, husband of their dear niece, Lucy, whom Gladstone called 'the son of my right hand', had just been brutally murdered in

Ireland. Both William and Catherine were deeply shaken but then William's self-control reasserted itself and Catherine's thoughts turned to helping others, especially Lucy. Nevertheless, the shock of the tragedy aged them both visibly. Once again it was William's career that restored Catherine's zest for life. By the end of the 1880s she accompanied him everywhere. A spectator remembered seeing them both at a meeting in Marylebone. 'He is followed by a simply-dressed woman who busies herself in warding off the hands of enthusiasts ready to touch him. This is Mrs Gladstone, with the soft face, high-coloured like a girl's, and tremulous mouth, intent on one thing only in this life – her husband.' The extent to which this was so is reflected in a story told about her and a pious lady visitor with a pressing theological problem. 'What a comfort to know there is One above who is able to tell us!' sighed the visitor. 'Yes, William should be down in a few minutes,' a completely straight-faced Catherine replied.

1889 was the year of the Gladstones' golden wedding anniversary. Presents poured in from the rich and powerful, including a monumental silver-gilt inkstand from the Prince of Wales. The family's present was a new stone porch for the castle door at Hawarden. It replaced the rickety wooden contraption, which they had christened 'the bathing-machine'. For Catherine, 'the only cloud on a perfect golden sunset' was the illness of her eldest son, Willy. For a while he improved but then the doctors discovered a brain tumour. Catherine's letter to William when he died is a quiet acceptance of death. She thought of his grief rather than hers, although she was always closest to Willy. But now that she was in her late seventies, she could accept things more philosophically. And she still kept her capacity for looking forward. There were still others to be helped. In December 1893 she wrote to William, 'Was glad I went by train, was of some use trying to comfort a hysterical woman.' And there was William's career to strive for, though he was now deaf and failing in one eye. The country called him the Grand Old Man and Catherine herself was *Grande Dame*.

Right till the very end, she willed him to stay in office. As her daughter, Mary, was later to write, 'All Mama's heart is fixed on him remaining in Parliament.' He may have felt he had a duty to Ireland but there is no doubt she helped to keep him in power long after he would and *should* have retired. But she could not change the inevitable and on 2 March 1894 she accompanied him to Windsor to hand in his resignation. Morley had had to break the news to her as Gladstone could not bring himself to do it. 'The poor old lady,' he wrote, 'I was breaking to her that the pride and glory of her life was at last facing eclipse.' By 12 March she was leaving Downing Street, tearfully bidding the staff goodbye. Mary Gladstone summed up her mother's feelings over the past few years. 'You know how she loves being inside the main spring of history and all the stir and stress and throb of the machine is life and breath to her.' Her older sister, Agnes, agreed: 'Mama lived a hundred lives at one go.'

Gladstone had no recognition from the Queen though she would no doubt have given him a peerage had he wanted one. Catherine was entitled to an extinct barony in her own right and was asked if she would like to claim it. But she refused, inevitably. Any other name but Gladstone was unthinkable.

William's retirement years passed more happily than Catherine's. He had his theological and classical studies to absorb him. She resented especially being dependent on others. 'I long to give less trouble and visit the poor.' But when William's eye operation proved successful, they could at least do more things together. They visited

France and Germany and distinguished visitors flocked to Hawarden from many different walks of life – including Burne-Jones and the Prince of Wales.

In the autumn of 1897 William developed signs of a serious illness which quickly showed itself to be cancer of the palate. At first he longed for an easy death until he thought about leaving Catherine. Then, 'I shall ask no more for instant dismissal.' In March 1898 he arrived for the last time at Hawarden. Catherine did not leave his side again and was kneeling beside him when he died. By this time her mind was clouding over but miraculously it was quite clear during the funeral. In the midst of her own grief and loneliness she heard of a man killed on the Hawarden estate and insisted on driving to see the widow, kneeling to pray with her on her cottage floor.

Her dignity and bearing astonished the crowds who watched the funeral. Silent working people in black lined the funeral route from Hawarden church to the railway station. The entire congregation of Westminster Abbey rose as one when she entered, still a graceful figure, at the great west door. Among the pall-bearers were the Prince of Wales, the future Edward VII and Prince George, later George V as well as old friends and colleagues. At the end of the service the Prince of Wales stooped to kiss her hand.

Her last two years were, perhaps mercifully, lived in twilight. She retreated further and further into the past except when visitors came to talk of William. At the end of May 1900 she caught a mild cold and then pneumonia. Life flickered on for a while but she did not really want to live. She died in the house where she was born on the evening of 14 June 1900. Three days later she was buried next to her beloved William. It was all she had ever wanted.

Mrs Disraeli, later Lady Beaconsfield,
engraved by W. H. Mote
after the portrait by A. E. Chalon

Mrs Gladstone
in the first year of her marriage,
by F. R. Say

Mrs Asquit
later Lady Oxford and Asquit
in 192

Mrs Lloyd George,
photographed by Ernest Mills

Mrs Asquith

When Arthur Balfour, the future Prime Minister, was reputed to be contemplating marriage to Margot Tennant, he scotched the rumour immediately by saying, 'No, that is not so. I rather think of having a career of my own.' Instead, the ambitious, gifted Margot caught another prime minister – 'my PM' as she called Herbert Asquith possessively – and a more unlikely match would have been hard to find. Even Queen Victoria was scandalized at the choice of her solemn, young Home Secretary and pronounced Margot 'unfit for a Cabinet Minister's wife'.

Her reasons were easy to understand. Most of the older members of the establishment tended to agree with her. Margot had made a name for herself in Victorian England as a brazen, spoiled society darling – brilliant, waspish, indiscreet, theatrical to the point of being vulgar. She and her small, exclusive circle of gilded, talented youth – 'the souls' as they were known semi-humorously to outsiders – were defying convention and changing the face of 'Society' even before it was due to be changed for ever with the outbreak of the First World War. Ironically, this was not something they set out to do deliberately or even consciously. Margot and her equally lionized sister, Laura, who married Alfred Lyttelton, were not so much challenging the status quo as displaying their genuine ignorance of how London society worked.

They themselves had had an extraordinary upbringing for the period, running free and wild in the grounds of their Scottish home. It was an ideal place to be a child: no wonder they could not imagine any other, more formal way of life.

The Tennant family had made its fortune by founding a chemical works in Glasgow, which at one point, was the largest in the world. They were solid, provincial Scottish businessmen living in a bleak Glasgow mansion. It took an adventurer like Margot's father Charles to turn his back on this limited life and open the doors for his family to society, politics and the arts. In the process he himself, a staunch Liberal, was created a baronet on Gladstone's recommendation.

Charles's first move was the building of Glen, a Scottish baronial fantasy in the Peebleshire hills. Like others before him, he recognized that, although riches conferred respectability, to be a true gentleman required a country estate. Nevertheless, he never quite became used to the extent of his good fortune: late at night, by the light of a candle, he would surreptitiously inspect his treasured collection of Romneys, Reynolds and Raeburns, as if to make sure they were still there.

Among the few things in life he valued more were his bevy of exceptional daughters. His sons, although good-hearted boys, were growing up in the conventional mould of the English squire. Like their timid mother they were totally eclipsed by these bright, vital beings – passionate, quarrelsome, highly intelligent and intimately devoted to each other. Margot and her closest sister, Laura, even dressed alike. Mary Catherine Gladstone's daughter, summed up a visit to the Glen household: 'I have had the strange, rather mad experience of the Tennant circle. I couldn't describe it – it is the maddest merriest whirl from morn till night – wonderful quickness, brightness, wit, cleverness – the 4 sisters all so fascinating in their different ways.' Others were less impressed. Their brothers said they were 'more like lions than sisters'. The coachman's wife at Glen called Margot 'a little Turk'. Her nurses, trained to be more tactful, spoke of 'a venturesome child'. Significantly, the last one left when her charge was still only ten years old. Left to her own devices, Margot became uncontrollable. She climbed the precipitous roof of the house by moonlight; she rode her pony up the front steps. Every day she roamed the moors which stretched up to the walls of the garden. There, she boasted, she knew 'every clump of heather'. As a result, she missed whatever chance she had of an education. Only her own interest and her father's magnificent library saved her from being almost illiterate. As it was, Dr Jowett, the Master of Balliol, called her 'the best educated ill-educated woman that I have ever met'. Yet, although lacking in application, Margot was gifted with exceptional facility. She could draw well, play the violin beautifully and play tennis as well as any man. Constantly driving herself on, she was impatient with non-achievers who could not *do* things. There is a famous story of her in conversation with a frail and fey young woman.

'What do you do?' enquired Margot peremptorily, to which the reply came, 'I don't do anything.'

'What can you do?'

A hesitant pause. 'I can't do anything.'

Sighing with exasperation and disgust, Margot turned abruptly on her heel. 'Go out and kick a hat!' she cried.

Along with a marked insensitivity, Margot had unbridled egotism. Nobody ever thought her more fascinating, or her remarks wittier, than she did herself. It is arguable that the only relationship in her life, not based on self-interest, apart from that with her son, was her genuine, deep intimacy with her beloved sister, Laura. Until Laura's marriage at the age of 23 in 1885, the two sisters slept together in the night nursery in small, child-size beds – with 'only a brass railing and knobs'. Here Margot remembered them 'reading together, praying together, laughing and crying together' as well as 'discussing life, lovers, letters and literature'. They once argued about imagination until 8 a.m. when the housemaid came in to wake them up.

Together, also, in 1881, they were launched on London society, an inauspicious debut that involved much standing against walls in brand-new ballgowns. Laura, at least, was asked to dance occasionally. Margot had no illusions about her own lack of physical appeal. 5 feet 2 inches, skinny, flat-chested, with a large, bony face – 'I have no face, only two profiles clapped together' – she had to be allowed to talk before she could dazzle.

And at last she was. By dint of strenuous politicking, she managed to obtain vouchers for the Royal Enclosure at Ascot. She met the Prince of Wales there, and typically, 'I felt my spirits rise.' After that the invitations flooded in to her father's splendid house in Grosvenor Square. As Laura recorded on 8 May 1883 in her diary: 'Who could help being conquered by [Margot] – she carries victory in her eyes.' And indeed, the voluble Tennant sisters made a tremendous impact on the stale society of the early 1880s. They brought new blood, new life, even the art of conversation back to the endless round of elaborately-ordered dinner parties and trivial, gossipy afternoon teas. 'General conversation!' Margot would demand, emphatically banging the dinner table, and she and Laura would swop pencilled notes on menu cards as to what topics to introduce next.

Round this nucleus a group emerged of like-minded and equally talented young people – Curzon, Arthur

Balfour and Alfred Lyttelton among them. They were borne off to stay at Glen, where they monopolized the 'Doo' cot', Laura and Margot's sitting-room, to talk of art and literature or play intellectual games with pen and paper, far into the night. All this at a time when no respectable girl would stir without a chaperone. Even Margot bowed to convention in London and went to parties escorted by her brother, although they left separately and carried different latch-keys.

From these conversations, the nickname 'Souls' arose. 'You are always talking about your souls,' claimed Lord Charles Beresford. 'I shall call you the Souls.' It came to be used as the definitive term for what was only a loosely connected group of individuals. But the 'Souls' *en masse* had one important effect: they made it possible to be both political opponents and friends. Arthur Balfour was a Tory; the Tennants were passionately Liberal; Alfred Lyttelton, Gladstone's nephew, began as a Liberal and changed. Yet they saw each other more often than anyone else in their own parties. 'Till you and your friends appeared in London Society,' said Gladstone to Margot, 'men of different political convictions seldom spoke to one another unless they met at Court.' He himself was confronted with Lord Randolph Churchill over lunch at Margot's, after they had quarrelled violently in the House. Needless to say, they conversed quite amicably.

Like Lady Palmerston, Margot liked her guests to be of every political hue. She was not so much interested in political issues as in the prospect of a contest between great men. As with everything else, she saw politics in terms of absolutes, a simple matter of win or lose, in which her star was hitched firmly to the winner. Quite early on she told her father's friend, Mr Gladstone, that she wished to be a prime minister's wife 'like Aunt Pussy'. He replied soothingly that he was sure she would make a splendid prime minister's wife – or any other kind.

But this time, it was Laura who was to be married, and to the Gladstones' nephew, Alfred Lyttelton. Margot was pleased for her, but conscious of the gap it would leave in her life. 'I can't help it, it may be selfish,' she wrote to her friend, George Curzon, 'but it's true I *mind* Laura going, she's part of myself and I shall shriek at the empty bed now and work off what I've wanted to say by biting my pillow and burying my head, no one, no one takes that place, say what you like, 21 years just we two in the most perfect closest intimacy . . .' It was a letter written in Margot's inimitable, highly emotional, breathless style.

By 1887, Laura was expecting a baby. So close were the sisters that Margot was sent to the country in case she became upset. She was hunting with the Beaufort hunt on a sunny Saturday in April 1888 when she took one of her innumerable tumbles, and ended up, bruised and slightly concussed, in bed. She was still recovering when the news was brought to her that Laura, having given birth to a son, was gravely ill. Nothing the doctors said could restrain Margot from going to her immediately. Still shaky with shock, she made the journey to London by train. She was there holding her sister's hand when she died.

At the age of twenty-four Margot felt that a large part of her life was over. She wrote later, 'My sister Laura's death had more effect on me than any event in my life, except my own marriage and the birth of my children.' Her life now became even more hectic and restless, her conversation noticeably barbed and brittle. Despite her egocentricity she had always been highly-strung and nervous. There was no one now with whom she could totally relax. It marked the start of the insomnia which was to plague her for the rest of her life.

She worked off much of her phenomenal restlessness on the hunting-field. Few riders, wrote Winston Churchill, were 'able to surpass this featherweight daredevil, mounted upon enormous horses, who with faultless nerve and thrust and inexhaustible energy, spurred by love of chase and desire to excel, came sometimes to grief but always to the fore'. A friend once made a tally of her injuries. In a few years she broke her nose, her ribs, one knee-cap and both her collar-bones at different times. She also suffered a fractured skull, a dislocated jaw and five minor concussions of the brain. 'I am not afraid of suffering too much in life,' she once remarked airily, 'but much more afraid of feeling too little.' In the same vein she continued, 'I prefer a heart on a sleeve to a heart on a shelf.'

She herself, over the past few years, had worn her heart conspicuously on her sleeve for one man. To make it all the more poignant, he was a man she knew within herself neither wanted nor deserved it. Peter Flower was a dashing, charming wastrel, a superb rider but singularly lacking in brains. Even Margot was compelled to joke about his 'shoot 'em down' solutions to industrial disputes. His greatest joy, apart from hunting, was playing elaborate practical jokes while he lived by taking on foolhardy bets with his friends. Nevertheless, Margot waited nine years for him to declare himself, a triumph of patience and perseverance for someone who once announced she found most 'oratory, biography, operas, films, plays, books, and persons, too long'. Admittedly, her name was linked simultaneously with those of several other men, but when stirred, she was capable of great loyalty. She had shown it once and she would show it (when she married Asquith) again.

Yet society saw only her apparent fickleness as she played off one man against another. Margot loved being the centre of attention. It was her *raison d'être* to be a *cause célèbre*. She was a self-made social phenomenon just as the Tennants were self-made millionaires. In any case, she did little to deny the rumours of romances, although to the other party it sometimes came as an unwelcome shock. 'Does Miss Margot contradict her reported marriage?' pondered Sir Henry Ponsonby as yet another 'engagement' hit the headlines. 'I think she has been married by newspaper report to all the bachelors and widowers in the government.' Arthur Balfour could take it in his stride, but Lord Rosebery was offended and cooled towards his former friend. Margot, typically, was unrepentant.

In fact, a large portion of Margot's affection seems to have been reserved for much older men. Her father was William Gladstone's friend, but so was she. He loved to hear her talk and once wrote her a poem. She wrote back to thank him: 'You must allow me to say that you are ever such a dear.' In 1889 Margot went to stay at Hawarden and wrote a description of Gladstone's library, published later in *Cornhill* magazine. The Gladstones paid a return visit to Glen the following year. Dr Jowett of Balliol was another correspondent. He lectured her severely on frittering away her talents. 'She might be a distinguished authoress if she would,' he wrote in a pen sketch of her, 'but she wastes her time and her gifts scampering about the world and going from one country house to another in a manner not pleasant to look back upon and still less pleasant to think of twenty years hence, when youth will have made itself wings and flown away.' Margot, chastened for once, wholeheartedly agreed. 'Too many interests and too many-sided . . . Great want of plodding perseverance, doing many things with promise and nothing well.' She was as ruthless with herself as she was with others.

She was, however, trying to discipline herself to become a writer. At Glen she had masterminded the publication of a schoolroom newspaper, *The Glen Gossip*. Now, she attempted to start a literary newsletter for general circulation. Various friends promised to contribute, including Oscar Wilde, Ellen Terry, Wilfred Blunt and Sir Edward Burne-Jones as well as the ubiquitous Arthur Balfour. But 'To-morrow', as it was to be called, never came. Perhaps the first serious article she wrote was her description of a trip to Egypt in 1891. Her parents took her there as a last resort to 'save her from marrying a hunting man', in other words, Peter Flower. She visited Wilfred Blunt in the Egyptian desert, attended the Khedive's strange and splendid funeral, was continually disgruntled and longed to return home. When she did, she met Henry Asquith.

Ironically, the meeting took place at a dinner given by Peter Flower's brother. 'I had never heard of him,' Margot later commented sardonically, 'which gives some indication of how much I was wasting my time.' She remembered being impressed by Asquith's conversation and 'Cromwellian face', and the horror inspired by his unfashionable, baggy clothes. She herself was always dressed in the height of fashion.

They met again at a House of Commons official banquet shortly before he became the Liberal Home Secretary. Obviously destined for high office though he was, Asquith lived a scholarly and retiring life in Hampstead. Margot, in the patronizing way she had towards 'the middle classes', decided it would be amusing to adopt her unassuming new friend and 'bring him out'. She did not realize at first that he was married, but in any case she had never contemplated matrimony with a man of his kind. When, after his first wife died, Asquith did propose to her, it took her several years to accept. For the present, she liked what she saw of Helen Asquith, so 'gentle, pretty and unambitious, and spoke to me of her home and children with love and interest that seemed to exclude her from a life of political aggrandizement which was from early days the life that captivated my imagination . . . When I said that she had married a man who was certain to attain the highest political distinction, she replied that that was not what she coveted for him.' Asquith himself spoke of his first wife with solicitude and affection but admitted later that she was a 'restricting rather than a stimulating influence'. Had she lived she might well have become a liability for, even before he met Margot, Asquith's success was opening new doors. Besides attending House of Commons banquets, he was being taken up by fashionable hostesses and invited for dinners and weekends, almost always without his wife. Helen, like him, came from a solid, provincial Midlands family, but unlike him did not have the wish to adapt. As it was, she was not long for this world. She died of typhoid in September 1891, leaving Asquith with five children between twelve years and eighteen months to clothe and feed in his Hampstead house.

Already he was captivated by Margot. 'Good and sweet beyond words', he called her, although these are not two of her qualities that spring to mind, especially as she was leading him such a merry dance. 'I dread more than I can tell having to go back . . . to where we were two months ago,' he wrote after a particularly trying time in summer 1892. But shortly afterwards his spirits rose again: 'This afternoon as I sat on the Treasury bench, answering questions, I got your telegram and read it furtively, and crammed it hastily into my trousers pocket, until I could get out of the House and read it over and over again in my little room.'

'Never doubt,' he wrote, telling her of his feelings, 'that, locked and buried though it may be, your place is always sacred and always your own . . .'

His friends were able to accept what they deemed a short-lived infatuation. But when marriage rumours began to circulate, they were, almost without exception, appalled. Lord Rosebery even went so far as to suggest that such a match would ruin Asquith's promising political career. Lord Randolph Churchill, although insisting that he liked Margot, agreed with him. They could not believe that this frivolous, magpie-minded creature of society could be taken seriously as a hard-working politician's wife. Shortly before Margot's engagement was announced, a novel was published with a heroine who purported to be based on her. Called *Dodo*, it was written by E. F. Benson, son of the Archbishop of Canterbury. It was about 'a pretentious donkey with the heart and brains of a linnet', commented Margot, breezily dismissing the book. But others took it more seriously. A friend whom Asquith went to stay with left it conspicuously on his bedside table. In a most unAsquithian gesture of fury he flung it out of the window into the flower-bed below.

Even face to face, Margot was subjected to prophecies of doom and disaster. She remembered a particular occasion at a Downing Street dinner, when the 'political wives' led by 'dear old Mrs Gladstone' began hinting darkly about the duties of a possible prime minister's wife. Having heard that she must be prepared to give up acting, dancing and riding, Margot, her 'nerves racing round like a squirrel in a cage', sought comfort from Gladstone himself. This he was never able to deny her, though even he added cautiously that it would be a mistake not to turn criticism to good account.

In any case, Margot was honest and perceptive enough to have her own misgivings. Asquith had no background, no country house, no money – except for what he earned as a barrister – and no entrée into society. What he did have was a ready-made family of dauntingly intelligent and precocious children. Among Margot's smart hunting set – 'the good-humoured, ill-educated people with whom I spent my winters' – he would have been regarded as donnish and eccentric. So austere was he personally that he shunned modern innovations like heating and telephones, and could never be persuaded to part with his beloved quill pen. He was sturdily built but took little exercise. Once when Margot urged him to run to catch a train, he refused: 'I don't run much.'

Yet something in Margot, 'some unstifled inner voice', as she described it, told her she would be 'untrue to myself and quite unworthy of life if, when such a man came knocking at the door, I did not fling it wide open . . .' And so, in spring 1894 she accepted him, two and a half years after he had first proposed to her and in the year she was 30 and he was 41. She left in her wake a trail of rejected suitors, casualties of countless love affairs in ten reckless, fickle London seasons. But she would never waver in her loyalties again. 'You are going to marry one of the finest men in the world . . . such a man is a companion that any woman might envy you,' wrote John Morley to her, and she never disputed it. 'Asquith is the only kind of man that I could ever have married,' she reflected later, 'all the others are so much waste paper!'

Asquith's second wedding was very different from his first in Manchester seventeen years earlier. It was a glittering affair at which three Prime Ministers, besides the bridegroom, signed the register: Gladstone represented the past, Rosebery the present and Arthur Balfour, the future. The streets around St George's, Hanover Square were blocked with anxious and excited spectators while the Cabinet postponed a meeting for it on Asquith's personal request. He was Home Secretary now and 'the man of the future' in the Liberal camp.

Autumn 1894 found the Asquiths installed at 20, Cavendish Square, a roomy, rambling house bought with Tennant money. They were to remain there, except for the years in Downing Street, until 1920. Margot would never have considered living anywhere as unfashionable as Hampstead. It was a comfortable house upstairs but the back quarters were inconvenient. The food had to be carried from the mews kitchen across an open courtyard. Margot, being Margot, saw that they had the staff to maintain it: fourteen servants including a butler and two footmen as well as a coachman and stable boy. They needed them, too, with lunch and dinner parties every day. 'I hope to die in debt,' was one of the rules by which Margot lived.

Such extravagance was all very well when Asquith was still in office as a minister, but in 1895, the Liberal government fell. With no salary, huge expenses, and four sons to educate, the former Home Secretary had to return to the bar. It marked a break with tradition on the part of a recently deposed cabinet minister but at least now he could rely on a regular income of £5000–£10,000 a year, enough to maintain Margot's hunting horses and rent a house every summer in Scotland. Margot's father, after his initial generosity, had not made any further financial contributions. He was too preoccupied with his new, young, second wife. At the age of seventy-five, he had married Marguerite Miles, a thirty-year-old Englishwoman and proceeded to father three daughters in succession. Margot, at first rather shocked by the prospect of a step-mother four years younger than her, soon became quite fond of Marguerite. There were emotional scenes of reconciliation at Glen in a room full of weeping Tennants. But the marriage had 'made it clear that we can't hope for anything from [Papa]'. Or so she thought. In fact, she had misjudged her father. He continued to help her discreetly and eventually settled £5000 a year on her for life, so that Asquith could be relieved of his worst financial worries. But not yet.

In Cavendish Square, the Asquith step-children were installed on the upper floors. Margot had rescued them from exile in the country. She had met Violet, Asquith's only daughter, when they became engaged, and seen the others once, briefly, before her marriage. They were not what she had expected at all, a totally different breed from the Tennants. Remembering 'the storms of revolt, the rage, the despair, the wild enthusiasms and reckless adventures of our nursery and schoolroom', she had foreseen a similar sort of disruption to her own house. Instead, the Asquiths were cool, quiet, self-absorbed, rarely quarrelled or indeed showed any emotion. Their favourite form of relaxation was compiling intellectual quizzes with which they plied unsuspecting guests. They themselves were strikingly clever, especially Raymond and Violet. Arthur was the most competent, Herbert the most poetically gifted, and Cyril, 'the shyest and rarest', Margot's favourite. But she was noticeably kind and generous to them all, and as children, they adored her. She would sweep gaily into the nursery, at any time of the day, upsetting the cherished routine, scandalizing the nursemaids with her tales of murders and ghosts, planning the games of charades that she loved as much as the children themselves. 'She filled us,' recalled Violet later, 'with admiration, amazement, amusement, affection, sometimes even with a vague sense of uneasiness as to what she might, or might not do next.' And indeed, once at Downing Street, the German governess burst in on Violet: 'Violet, Violet, come quickly! Mama is dancing in front of the new secretary in her combinations!' In fact, Margot had dressed up in the unfortunate butler's clothes to practise her disguise for the children's Christmas party. She teased all the Asquiths unmercifully, calling them 'skeletons with brains' and berating them for their seemingly endless ability to sleep. She herself was often too nervous to eat or sleep. 'All Asquiths sleep like hogs,' she observed despairingly in her diary, and then in a fit of compunction changed the '*hogs*' to '*logs*'.

The bond of affection between Margot and his children did much to take the weight of fatherhood off Asquith's shoulders. Secure in the knowledge that she would love and care for them, he could concentrate on his career: his 'great and solemn career', as Margot called it almost reverently. It remained her one constant interest in an overcrowded, restless life. Everything else – hunting, music, drawing, even, for a time, golfing, went by the board.

Asquith himself took it as his due that he would one day be leader of the Liberal party. As Home Secretary, in a fragmented Liberal government, he had proved a noted success. Ironically, by staying aloof from faction, he had won his own personal following. Now he was content to wait and let time and events take him to the top.

Margot, ambitious though she was for him, was incapacitated for much of this vital period. In May 1895 after a miscarriage she was prostrated for three months with phlebitis. In all out of five pregnancies, three ended in miscarriage and in each case after the full nine months had been run. One daughter and one son were, after much trouble, delivered safely. Elizabeth was born in 1897, while Anthony followed in 1902. But the effect on Margot's over-strung nerves was to induce almost total insomnia. 'No one who has not experienced over any length of time real sleeplessness can imagine what this means . . . insomnia is akin to insanity,' she said. By 1908 she was worn out, and according to her autobiography, greeted the news of her husband's premiership by going to St Paul's Cathedral to pray 'that I might die rather than hamper his life as an invalid'. It was a typically exaggerated Margot episode – or fantasy as the case may be.

Before he achieved the premiership, Asquith served as Chancellor in a Liberal government of which Sir Henry Campbell-Bannerman was the token leader. He was elderly and ailing, and even the outspoken Margot could not resent him. 'C.B.,' she wrote in 1905, 'is not young or very strong and is not likely to prove a formidable rival, he is devoted to H. and is a dear old thing . . .' Besides, while in the Exchequer, Asquith had the chance to produce two important budgets, one of which established the principle of old-age pensions. Margot was proud and pleased, though not because of his social policies. She went to the Commons to hear him speak. 'No one speaks quite like Henry. He seems to run rather a bigger show; he can keep to the ground, cut into it or leave it without ever being ridiculous, boring or wanting in taste, and he is never too long. He gives a feeling of power rather than of grace or charm.' For her, he was coming into his own. She had always courted great men.

The Chancellor's family were not living in Number 11, Downing Street. Margot had rejected it as too small for their needs. Certainly, it had no clearly designated nursery or schoolroom, although it is doubtful whether Margot would have had to 'farm out' her children as she maintained. In any case, Sir Charles Tennant made it possible for them to refuse it, by offering the equivalent of the rent they could have asked for Cavendish Square. Thankfully, Margot stayed where she was. Herbert Gladstone, the new Home Secretary, moved into Number 11.

In February 1908, Campbell-Bannerman had a heart attack. He never returned to the House, nor indeed ever left his room again. Asquith was heir-apparent to the leadership but before he could form a government, he had to be asked by the King, who was holidaying in Biarritz. On 14 April he left London by train, very quietly, said Margot, with a travelling cap pulled down over his eyes. A few days after his arrival in Biarritz a letter reached Cavendish Square. It was as dry and factual as such a letter could be, totally unlike the emotional, highly-coloured ramblings of his wife. '[The King] said "I appoint you P.M. and First Lord of the Treasury" whereupon I knelt down and kissed his hand. *Voilà tout*! . . . I leave at 12 noon to-morrow and arrive Charing Cross 5.12 Friday afternoon. You will no doubt arrange about dinner that evening . . .' Margot did more than that. She waited with the crowds on the station platform although it was bitterly cold and she had recently been ill. The cheering and the excitement did as much as anything to make her well again.

Early in May 1908, nine Asquiths moved into Number 10. 29 year-old Raymond was now a barrister, and about to be married from Number 10 three months later; Arthur was a businessman, Herbert a writer and Cyril, at seventeen, had not yet decided on a career. Violet hovered on the brink of her first real London season, for which Margot spent a fortune on dresses from Monsieur Worth. Margot's own children, Elizabeth and Anthony (Puffin) were, at eleven and five, still in the nursery. The family were to remain in Number 10 for 8½ years, during which time they made it less of an office and more of a home. It could not have been anything else with the entire Asquith brood encamped on the third floor. Sometimes, also, Margot's three tiny half-sisters came to stay, the offspring of her father's late second marriage. One of them, Katharine, Lady Elliot, can remember the house resounding to the sound of children's parties, the secretaries for once banished to the offices on the lower ground floor. Later on in the suffragette period, the upper windows would be filled with children, sometimes throwing things at the unfortunate women chained to the railings below. The policemen, plagued by Anthony's aeroplanes, which swooped over the garden wall without warning, actually formed a deputation to complain.

No family had really used the house since the Gladstones left it fourteen years earlier. Rosebery was a widower, Balfour a bachelor, the Campbell-Bannermans old and ill, while the Salisburys chose to live elsewhere. Margot found it unequipped for entertaining: 'It is an inconvenient house with three poor staircases and after living there a few weeks I made up my mind that owing to the impossibility of circulation I could only entertain my Liberal friends at dinner or at garden-parties.' It was partly an affectation that she had made up her mind to dislike the house. 'Liver-coloured and squalid', was how she described the outside of it. At any rate, she inaugurated an ambitious programme of improvements, dragging the reluctant Board of Works in her wake. She even managed to install an electric lift, although for the first few years of its life it seldom worked.

This done, Margot began the inevitable round of political dinner parties, though hers were spiced with interesting personalities and figures from the arts. Jo Grimond, another Liberal leader and married to Violet's daughter, Laura, recently compared this era at Downing Street with the White House under Kennedy. At the centre of all the dash and brilliance, there was a shrewd, political purpose. Among Margot's prime considerations was her husband's career. The most frequent invitations went to the up-and-coming young men of the Liberal party, who were 'captured' like prize booty for the Asquith camp. Winston Churchill was an *habitué* at Margot's parties as were Edwin Montagu, Asquith's secretary, and the left-wing trade-unionist, John Burns. The atmosphere was always stimulating and sometimes turbulent. Often, Margot arbitrarily mixed guests from both political parties. A Liberal Runciman might find himself sitting next to a Tory Chamberlain and having to forget the animosity of years.

As Prime Minister in the pre-war period, Asquith was anything but overworked. He took time off for long holidays in Scotland, where for the past few years he had rented a house. Archerfield, near North Berwick, had the attraction of its own private golf course. Asquith played on it daily, accompanied by his wife, who braved the Scottish winds in an exquisite but unsuitable French silk dress. 'Golf was the only thing,' said her half-sister Katharine, 'that Margot ever did badly.' It did not stop her trying, though.

In July 1912, the Asquiths decided to buy a country house of their own. The Wharf at Sutton Courtenay near Abingdon, had begun life as an inn. It stood near the river behind a derelict, timbered barn. It was small, pokey and even when converted, unprepossessing, but Margot somehow managed to cram it full of life. Crowds of assorted guests would descend for weekend parties – 'the menagerie' as Asquith rudely called them. In fact, he presided over such weekends with considerable enjoyment so long as his own routine was not disturbed. He would play golf on Saturday, lunching often at Skindles, Maidenhead, and arrive back at the Wharf in the evening in time to dine. The dining-room would be smoky, noisy and packed to capacity. Margot once had to call in a builder to try to deaden the din Her voice always stood out, low-pitched and harsh-timbred; as she spoke, she gesticulated wildly with her bony, heavily-ringed hands. At the other end of the table Asquith revelled in the incongruity of the guest-list. He recalled with glee the spectacle of Pierpont Morgan seated between Elizabeth and the German governess. It was partly to amuse him that Margot chose her friends, in any case. She was conscious of his dislike of society women with 'lending-library minds . . . There is a sort of nonstop stupidity among the upper classes which I find exceedingly exhausting'. As a politician, Asquith also detested talking politics. Margot's interesting and lively gatherings were the best relief he could have had.

Children who visited the Wharf were housed in the pretty Mill House across the village high street. Margot herself made her bedroom in the barn. Like Lloyd George she woke before dawn and would sit up in bed, scribbling furiously and smoking Turkish cigarettes, swathed in Shetland shawls. At breakfast her guests would be greeted with the fruit of her labours – imperious, pencilled notes, usually about their appearance the night before.

'Darling, I thought you looked terrible last night . . .' ran one, and another: 'Can I be your skin doctor?' Occasionally, there would be praise: 'Darling, what a pretty dress!'

By this stage Margot's marriage seems to have subsided into an easy companionship. She was devoted to Henry and he to her but she was not the only woman in his life. From 1912 until 1915, when she married Edwin Montagu, Asquith was in love with Venetia Stanley, a friend and contemporary of Violet's. Admittedly, their romance was mostly a postal one. He wrote her hundreds of letters, some in the midst of Cabinet meetings. But they did also manage frequent meetings 'To see you again,' he wrote to her, 'and be with you, and hear your voice . . . has made a new creature of me. You are the best and richest of life-givers.' When she married, it was a terrible blow to him. It took him a long time to forgive her, or Montagu, his friend. In fact, for Venetia, the marriage was probably an escape. To a young girl, the needs of a middle-aged man must have seemed a crushing emotional burden.

Venetia's marriage ended Asquith's only serious love affair but he had several other female confidantes. Lady

Scott, widow of the explorer, was one; Mrs Harrison another. He also wrote to Lillian Tennant, Margot's niece. The family joked about his 'leading ladies' but Margot insisted that, 'since I had known many men, I was anxious that my husband should have more friends among my sex'. She even maintained that she posted his letters to them, when she found them in the hall.

It may well have been true. Physical attraction had never played an important part in her feelings for Henry, unlike her relationship with the dashing Peter Flower. Of that she said, according to Herbert's wife, Lady Cynthia Asquith, 'I slept with him every night – every night of my life – everything except the thing itself.' Henry and Margot had other gifts to offer each other – friendship, companionship, constant mental stimulation, common political aims and a deep, ingrained loyalty. 'My life has been lived in full partnership with her,' wrote Asquith about his marriage, 'and all our experiences, both joy and sorrow . . . have been shared in common. By force of circumstance we have seemed to live much in the glare of publicity, but our true life has been elsewhere.' Besides, in middle age Margot found the question of sex 'wearisome'. 'Surprisingly,' she admitted, 'since [it] dominates the destinies of half mankind.' But 'all sense of fatigue disappears,' she wrote to her equally notorious contemporary, Nancy Astor, 'when Jane Austen takes us into her elegant and forgotten world . . . of love without sex.'

In 1914, Margot was fifty years old. Her husband, Henry, at nearly sixty-two, had been Prime Minister for over six years. They were together in Downing Street on 4 August, 1914, the night that war was declared. Margot recorded the expiry of the ultimatum in her autobiography. It was the sort of live drama that she loved:

'I joined Henry in the Cabinet room. Lord Crewe and

Sir Edward Grey were already there and we sat smoking cigarettes in silence; some went out; others came in; nothing was said.

'The clock on the mantelpiece hammered out the hour, and when the last beat of midnight struck it was as silent as dawn. We were at War.

'I left to go to bed and, as I was pausing at the foot of the staircase, I saw Winston Churchill with a happy face striding towards the double doors of the Cabinet room.'

It was a telling scene, except that her facts were wrong. The ultimatum expired at midnight in Germany, 11 p.m. London time.

Margot was rarely distressed or personally affected by the war. For her it was an exciting challenge, an adventure to be relished if not enjoyed. A friend she stayed with in the country remembered her reaction to a potentially lethal Zeppelin raid. 'It's very flat,' she commented disconsolately. 'Only one Zeppelin reached London and not a cat's been hurt.' Of course, although Asquith's son, Raymond, was killed along with many of her friends, she never suffered a great loss like so many other mothers and wives. Perhaps this was why she could be so heartless at times. She even accused her shell-shocked step-son, Herbert, of being drunk. '[Margot] has been here,' wrote his furious wife, Cynthia, in her diary, 'leaving a wake of weeping, injured people . . .' Asquith, she added, squeezed her hand, and 'looked at me with a tremendously charged expression intended to convey condolence on . . . the Margot affair'.

Probably Margot never intended to be cruel. She just said without thinking the first thing that came into her head. Even Lady Cynthia could not hate her for long. 'Poor Margot, her indiscretions are so naïve, so child-like . . . I always resent her so much more in theory than in practice.'

In any case Margot was not alone in her attitude

towards the war. To many of the English upper classes it came as an unwelcome shock to their easy way of life. But as the wife of the Prime Minister, Margot was in the public eye, and public opinion was outraged by her continued spendthrift entertaining. In 1915, Violet was married in a splendid society jamboree, 'the bridesmaids,' said Lady Cynthia, 'in velvet with gold toques . . . There is something terribly grim about a pompous wedding now. It seems so unnecessary and irrelevant, and one feels so remote . . .'

Lady Cynthia was doing war-work as a VAD, while in Number 11, Mrs Lloyd George, the wife of the Chancellor, was collecting funds for the troops. Margot did nothing. She had never much cared for social work, except after Laura's death when she took over her crêche in the East End. The poor were to be patronized, handed religion on a plate and rescued from the demon drink. Her attitude is not surprising when it is considered that at the age of sixteen she was allowed to hold Sunday-school 'classes' for the servants at Glen in the room of the middle-aged and highly respectable butler.

All this led to a campaign of vilification in the press. In a way, it was inevitable, for Margot had courted disaster. Naïvely, she let it be known that the war was not going to change her liking for Germans. As a result, a visit to a German POW camp was totally misconstrued. Before long, the country, in the grip of war hysteria, believed that Elizabeth was engaged to a German general, while Asquith had shares in Krupps. Behind some of the slanders was a sinister alliance of right-wing Tories, who accused Margot of perversion because Oscar Wilde's literary agent was among her friends. The jingoist, conservative Tory aristocracy was aghast at the idea of artists in Downing Street. They used the feeling in the country as an excuse to try to force the Asquiths out.

However, Asquith's unpopularity cannot all be blamed on Margot. If he had been a more successful war leader, he would have been able to withstand such attacks. As it was, he was indecisive, pessimistic, totally unwarlike. Venetia Stanley's defection had undermined his confidence: a friend remembered seeing him at the time of her marriage with 'a bruised look in his eyes'. After Raymond's death on the Somme, he withdrew even more into himself. Moody and unapproachable, he even missed Cabinet meetings. Meanwhile, by 1916, Lloyd George had come out into the open with his criticisms of the leadership. 'We are out,' confided Margot to her diary, 'it can only be a question of time.'

But whatever the outcome, she was determined to go down fighting. She struck back at Lloyd George whom she had never liked. He became the butt of her most trenchant witticisms: 'Lloyd George cannot see a belt without hitting below it.' . . . 'Put Lloyd George in a room by himself and he would shrivel up and disappear . . .' Lloyd George responded promptly in kind. 'Mrs Asquith,' he wrote to his wife, 'is silly . . . miserable and buzzes about like a mosquito in the room with her wings bedraggled but her sting active and indiscriminate.' To others of Henry's colleagues, Margot was absurdly personal. 'How can you find it in your heart to desert Henry,' she had written plaintively to Runciman, 'when Puffin has been such a friend of your little boy's.' Puffin was then fourteen and a schoolboy at Winchester. 'Twenty boys in poor Puff's bedroom,' his mother sympathetically remarked.

Late in 1916, the expected palace revolution took place. Asquith was ousted and Lloyd George headed a coalition of Liberals and Tories formed for the duration of the war. Asquith was left to lead a pathetic die-hard rump, all that remained of the once-glorious Liberal party. He was sixty-four and would never take office again. In fact, in

1918 he lost his East Fife seat and had to cast around for another one, until in 1924 he was made an earl. It was a humiliating end for a distinguished politician of the old school.

Fortunately, his was a resilient nature. By March 1917, he had recovered from the initial shock and was happily cataloguing his thousands of books 'into something like decent order'. And Margot remained indomitably vital. By now she had formed the habit of travelling third-class on trains, where – her critics said unkindly – she could be sure of a captive audience. 'Now, I am Mrs Asquith,' she would begin, 'and I expect you would like me to tell you something about my husband . . .'

It was very probable that she could not afford the first-class fare. Money was scarce now in the Asquith household. In spring 1920, they moved from Cavendish Square to Bedford Square in the cheaper district of Bloomsbury. Characteristically, Margot did not complain, but set to work at the age of fifty-six, to make her own fortune. In 1920, her best-selling autobiography was published. Inaccurate, melodramatic and indiscreet, it nevertheless had a candour and spontaneity that appealed to people. For the first time they read in print about the anguish of losing a still-born child. 'I wish,' commented an outraged dowager, 'she did not feel she must even publish her birth-pangs.' Margot herself disregarded the shocked criticism in the press, the embarrassment of her family and the horror of her friends. She had ears only for what Asquith might say. Diffidently, she left the first edition on his library table one night. She was in tears the next day when she heard him applaud it. 'I can say with truth that this has been the proudest moment of my life . . .'

As a result of his praise, she was spurred on to write. *More Memories*, *Off the Record* – the books followed in quick succession, all, it must be said, fairly similar to each other. Unfinished articles and character sketches littered her room in the barn. She even developed a morbid taste for compiling obituaries of her friends. Arthur Balfour, when she was staying with him, once picked up a random page. 'So Arthur Balfour is dead . . .' it began.

In 1922 she embarked on an American lecture tour but did not endear herself to the waiting millions by publishing a statement in the Pittsburgh press which read, 'The American female is a painted plaything.' At least one ladies' luncheon club cancelled its booking on the spot.

At home, Asquith was trying to emulate her success, and that of his colleague, Churchill, who in 1923 bought Chartwell with the proceeds from a book. He was anxious that, in accepting an earldom, he should have sufficient funds to keep it up. There was much derision over his choice of 'Oxford' for a title. One of the Cecils sneered, 'It is like a suburban villa calling itself Versailles.' He was obliged to change it to 'Oxford and Asquith' in any case when the Harley family protested to the College of Heralds.

A stroke in 1926 which temporarily incapacitated him was followed by another, more serious attack the following year. By October 1927 his mind was wandering and he had to be lifted in and out of a chair. Margot, who hated the idea of failure or suffering, was probably relieved to see the end. It came peacefully on a February evening in the cold winter of 1927–8.

The rest of her life was lonely, although she faced it with her customary fortitude, for most of her friends and contemporaries were already dead. She came to depend on her film director son, Anthony, with whom she lived in Bedford Square, and later in Kensington. The Wharf was sold immediately after Asquith's death.

Defying old age, beautifully dressed and over-rouged as always, she entertained and held soirées as she had done all her life. Artur Rubinstein once arrived to find the entire Diaghilev ballet corps in the drawing-room, with Margot dancing energetically in their midst. On summer evenings, crowds would gather outside her open windows to hear the famous musicians she frequently invited to perform.

She did not survive the Second World War, perhaps because she did not want to. It was a more unhappy time than any that had gone before in her life. Alone in the Savoy Hotel, where she was driven by sleepless nights as a result of the heavy bombing, she waited for the infrequent visits of her friends. Immersed in the war effort, they had little time to spare for a solitary old lady. Katherine, Margot's half-sister, was running the Land Army and could hardly see her at all.

Margot's one overwhelming sadness was her separation from her daughter, Elizabeth, who had married a Rumanian prince and was trapped there at the start of the war. Despairingly, her mother schemed to rescue her and kept her room ready in case, by some miracle, she should escape. Sadly, the reverse happened. In 1945, the news came that Elizabeth had died in Rumania. Heartbroken, Margot survived her by only a few months.

Dame Margaret Lloyd George

Criccieth in the 1870s: a small Welsh seaside resort, stifling in its respectability. Among the solemn, black-clad Sunday crowds treading the path between home and chapel, could be seen a 'little lad, attired in knicker-bockers and scarlet stockings, who time and again gave . . . the "glad eye" ' to a girl he passed on the main street. This is how, thirty or forty years later, Margaret Lloyd George was to remember her first meeting with her future husband.

She herself was one of the chapel-bound flock, escorted, no doubt, by her strict Calvinistic Methodist parents. Richard Owen, Margaret's father, who farmed on the hill above Criccieth, was one of the town's most worthy citizens. Rich by Welsh standards, he farmed a hundred acres and did not have to subsist on a diet of bread-and-dripping, turnips and potatoes like many of his neighbours. However, he was poorly educated and his wife could barely sign her name. Margaret was a cosseted only child, but she nevertheless remembered having to work hard with her mother in the kitchen, making cheese, melting down wax for candles, and scrubbing out the big old coal-fire range – although a village girl did come in to knead the bread. In winter the kitchen was the only comfortable room in any case, for there was no elecricity, gas or running water and no heating in the icy bedrooms.

Margaret's tiny, fiery mother and big, gentle father were fiercely Welsh and even more fiercely Puritan. Their daughter was disciplined with birch twigs, once for whistling on the Sabbath. But despite this her parents doted on her. Nothing was too good for her. She was sent off to boarding school for the education they had never had. Dr William's School for Girls was a genteel establishment thirty miles away, an immense distance to Margaret although her father customarily rode 300 miles to London. She travelled back and forth by train across the wooden railway bridge at Barmouth, much feared locally since the 1879 Tay Bridge disaster. She was happy there, but homesick for the bay at Criccieth with its twin castles and sweeping views of Snowdonia. She made the most of her holidays by learning to sail and paint.

In men and marriage she showed almost no interest until David Lloyd George began his pursuit of her in 1884. Admittedly, she was only eighteen and could safely have left such momentous decisions to the future, except that Lloyd George, now that he had found her again, was determined not to let her go. His diary of 10 June 1884 records the first signs of his renewed interest: 'Went to C[riccieth]. Maggie Owen . . . there. She is a sensible girl without any fuss or affectation about her.' Eleven days later he chaired the Debating Society's grand soirée, a red-letter event in the somewhat sparse Criccieth social calendar, and took Maggie Owen home, the 'short way' as befitted their short acquaintance. Presumably, there was also a 'long' way for less sheltered girls. From here on the friendship flourished. 'She seems to be a jollier girl as you get on with her,' observed Lloyd George.

But any thought of a formal courtship was out of the question for both families were vehemently opposed to the match. The Owens looked down on the struggling young solicitor who had been brought up by his cobbler uncle and still lived under his roof. He was too poor, too cheaply and flashily dressed and, considering his background, too noisily anti-establishment in the cases he chose to handle. The class of prosperous tenant farmers and lukewarm Liberals to which the Owens belonged, found him an annoyance and treated him as such, nicknaming him 'the bantam' for his small stature and aggressive political stance. But underneath they feared him, as they feared all those more radical than themselves.

Nor was David's uncle and mentor overjoyed at his choice. Richard Lloyd had taken his nephew in when he was fatherless and in need of a home. He had fed him, clothed him and seen to his education himself, poring over French and English, Latin and Greek, so that he could pass the knowledge on to 'his' boys. David and his brother William had been articled at appalling cost. They were still, in their early twenties, far from being able to stand on their own feet. No wonder Uncle Lloyd was aghast at the idea of any marriage at all, let alone David's choice of a Methodist bride. To ardent Baptists like the Lloyds, being a Methodist was not far removed from being the devil himself. Hurriedly Uncle Lloyd set about trying to distract his nephew with every available girl of his own class and creed.

In the end Lloyd George's sheer resourcefulness won the day: he hid his uncle's boots so that he could no longer shadow him about the streets; he left notes for Margaret in a secret hiding place in a stone wall; he cultivated the approval of her beloved and trusted aunt. And he grew more and more determined. 'Up to Mynydd Ednyfed' (the farm) ran his diary for 6 September 1886, 'and after knocking and dodging about in the rain for about a hour, I managed to whistle the servant girl out and she got Maggie for me.'

But by this time the biggest hurdle was Margaret's

own attitude. She was not sure how far she trusted his eloquent and easy tongue. She was fascinated certainly, and stimulated and amused, but she had her doubts as to whether he would ever make a good family man. With his dark good looks and persuasive blue eyes, Lloyd George already had a reputation as a philanderer and a flirt. Even his doting family had had occasion to reprimand him.

Faced with her hesitation, Lloyd George decided on attack rather than defence. 'Which would you prefer,' he challenged her, 'a namby-pamby who would always be hanging at the hem of your petticoat, or a real old demon, though he would sometimes lose his temper with you? Tell me the truth, old Maggie.' It was a sound piece of psychology. Despite the comparative hardship of a childhood in Wales, they had both been spoiled by a devoted family. Years of being the centre of attention had made them both equally proud and wilful and indeed this was a major part of the fascination they had for each other. Coming as she did from a home of rock-like security, Margaret was bound to be attracted by the streak of wildness in Lloyd George. By the end of 1886, Lloyd George felt confident enough to want to 'bring the matter to an issue . . . I somehow feel deeply that it is unmanly to take by stealth and fraud what I am honestly entitled to'. He prevailed upon her to accept his ring.

But all his cautious progress was undone when his name was linked with another Criccieth girl, one he had recently represented in a breach of promise action. Frigidly, Margaret wrote to suggest that he had perhaps made the wrong choice. He reacted, characteristically, by flinging back the gauntlet she had thrown down. 'I have made my choice . . . I must now ask you to make your[s] . . . we must settle this miserable squabble once and for all.'

They were married finally in January 1888 in a Methodist chapel in the pouring rain. To keep the peace, a Baptist minister was allowed to take part of the ceremony. Margaret became Margaret *Lloyd* George: her husband had added *Lloyd* to his surname as a tribute to his uncle. Afterwards the town celebrated with some unavoidably damp fireworks, but David and Margaret were already honeymooning in London. There they spent a week of true marital compromise, listening to Shakespeare one day, and the next, on Margaret's insistence, hearing sermons. Inevitably, there were rows: Lloyd George once threatened to fight a cab-driver and was only prevented when Margaret bodily intervened.

He was beginning to get the measure of the girl he had married. For all her feminine, gentle ways, Margaret had a will as strong as his own. Lloyd George believed that a wife's supreme function was 'to soothe and sympathize'. He expected his women to cater to his many vanities and fuss over his health and food, putting his needs before those of anyone else. This Margaret refused to do. Even when he became an MP, she was determined to live her own kind of life, even if it meant letting him go to London while she stayed behind in her beloved Wales. Inevitably, Lloyd George, with his need of women, looked to others to fill the gap. But the links with his wife were never broken. They met often in later years on common ground at their London house or when Lloyd George holidayed in Wales. Margaret was the only person who understood him without giving in to him. She was too honest and down-to-earth to be over-impressed by his meteoric rise. Nor did she hold the view that his genius excused his faults, particularly his self-centredness or the black vindictive moods which reduced most women to tears. As a result Lloyd George came to respect her proud, stubborn, independent spirit. He trusted her completely as he trusted no one else in his life. Their meetings were often stormy because she stood up to him, while elsewhere his word was law, but in many things he was anxious for her approval and went out of his way to try to win it. In particular, he attended chapel regularly even when he was alone in London, although Lloyd George was never anything but a pagan.

But for the moment these marital difficulties lay ahead. So did Lloyd George's career in politics, as now the 25 year-old solicitor and his 21 year-old bride settled down to live quietly with Margaret's parents in Criccieth. In 1889 Margaret gave birth to their first son, in the room where she herself had been born. Later, during her second pregnancy, her parents left their hilltop farm and built two solid, detached houses on the outskirts of the town. The Lloyd Georges then took possession of their first real home – but on a strictly commercial basis. Richard Owen was not prepared to waive a penny of rent for his unwelcome and highly unsuitable son-in-law.

For marriage had not softened Lloyd George's astringent tongue. On the contrary, he was more vociferously radical than ever. He had launched a Welsh nationalist and a socialist newspaper with a gift of £100 and was now seeking backing in order to stand for parliament. Such a project was not as ambitious as it sounds. At 26, Lloyd George was already a local alderman, 'the Boy Alderman', as the townspeople called him. In 1890 when the MP for Caernarvon Boroughs died, it seemed natural for him to stand as a Liberal against the Tory candidate. Not that he was expected to win. Ellis Nanney, the Tory, was exceptionally popular in the area and it was supposed that he would sweep the board before the young, untried radical. Nevertheless, Margaret's parents, still on the farm, received veiled threats from the neighbouring landlords, though neither they nor Margaret herself took any part in the campaign.

Margaret, in fact, dreaded the possibility that he might

win. 'I had thought,' she ruefully told a friend, 'I was marrying a Caernarvonshire lawyer.' When she heard about his nomination as a Liberal candidate, 'the shadow of the coming election spoilt everything . . . the sunshine seemed to have gone from the day.' With one child already, she worried about the future if Lloyd George should become a highly regarded but unpaid and virtually penniless MP. Moreover, she hated London, even what she had seen of it on honeymoon, while her love for Wales and Criccieth was one of the cornerstones of her life. She wanted nothing more than to remain there, living a quiet country life as a solicitor's wife. She almost had her way. The first count showed a Conservative victory. Only later was it announced that Lloyd George had scraped home by eighteen votes. The 'Boy Alderman' had become the 'Boy Member' for Caernarvon. He was to hold the seat for fifty-five unbroken years.

That night, 10 April 1890, Criccieth went wild in a frenzy of excitement. Bonfires blazed; every house was lit up. The normally staid townspeople went to cheer Lloyd George at Criccieth station, and accompanied his carriage in a torchlit procession through the streets. The noise of their shouts and singing could be heard well over a mile away. It brought an exasperated Margaret and her parents out to watch at the farmhouse door. From there they could see the exuberant crowds spilling up the steep hillside, but when they reached the farm gates, Margaret had had enough. She was too honest and forthright to be adept at dissembling her feelings and now all her anxiety and disappointment came to the fore. A nurse was sent out to tell them to stop the noise immediately. 'What is all this going on? . . . Do you want to wake the baby?' Stunned and subdued, the crowd melted away down the hill again while Lloyd George stepped into his father-in-law's house – alone.

He was still alone when he set off for London to take his place as a nervous new MP. Margaret came for a brief visit while he stayed with friends in an unglamorous part of Acton, but as soon as possible, she scuttled thankfully back to Wales. To be fair to her, it can be said that she was heavily pregnant and this was always the time when she hated London the most. With a deep-rooted and stubborn maternal instinct, she judged the city bad for her unborn child. So she was not in the House to hear her husband's first speeches, delivered timidly as if he was still uncertain of his command of English. It was only later when he had gained in stature and experience that the 'Welsh magician' enthralled the House with his fierce oratory.

He was now living in one room at the Liberal Club and had set himself up as a part-time solicitor in a tiny office in Gray's Inn Road. His first success came when he briefed a QC named Henry Asquith, one of the most eminent and most expensive in England. For this case Lloyd George received a fee of thirty guineas.

However, most of the time, money was short and there was now an additional mouth to feed. A daughter, Mair, had been born to Margaret in August 1890. The family was only saved by their interest in the Criccieth practice where brother William's hard work brought in substantial fees. Lloyd George, nominally a partner, collected the money but contributed very little. With typical egocentricity, he felt his political career came first.

However, his wife did not seem to think so. His 'dearest little round Maggie' as he called her, could not be dislodged from her life of comfortable motherhood in Wales. By dint of strenuous searching, Lloyd George had found rooms in Gray's Inn for the whole family at a manageable cost of £70 a year. He wrote early in 1891, begging Margaret to come. 'With a porter at the gate and two housekeepers on the premises and your own chambers double-doored and the windows iron-barred you surely ought to feel very secure until your husband comes home.' At last she arrived but with only one of the children as if to make clear this home was only a temporary one. And sure enough when May came, she disappeared to Wales for the rest of the summer, salving her conscience by sending back eggs, butter, flowers and fruit. When he remembered Lloyd George sent her his washing by return, but mostly he forgot: 'I haven't changed my drawers for a whole fortnight. Please send me a pair per parcel post.'

Throughout 1892 and 1893 Margaret was very rarely in London and Lloyd George, although increasingly lonely in 'that deserted . . . haunt of mine', was loath to visit Wales at the weekends. 'There is a great difference,' he wrote defiantly, 'between . . . being cramped up in a suffocating malodorous chapel listening to some superstitious rot . . . and [having] a ride on the river in the fresh air' – in this case at Kew. Already big-city living had exerted its fascination over him. He hated Criccieth's small-town atmosphere which he said was like living in a goldfish bowl.

1894 was no different except that Lloyd George, in financial difficulties, was obliged to move out of his newly-acquired Kensington flat. It was becoming an expensive business, running two places of residence. Out of a total annual income of £338 (minus £6 4s 7d tax), Lloyd George had to maintain, feed and clothe two households. By 1896, he had had enough. 'My bread is now so hard,' he wrote pitifully in March, 'that I could hardly cut it with the knife.' The flat 'has got into a very untidy state and no one would think of taking it'. This was followed by another broadside: 'We are spending more than we earn . . . unless I retire from politics altogether . . . we must give up the comforts of Criccieth for life in England.' But by this time, even if she had wanted to, Margaret could not come to him. She had had a miscarriage and her mother was ill.

To give her her due, her motives for staying away had never been wholly selfish. She genuinely wanted her four children to enjoy the benefits of a childhood in Wales. Lloyd George might fume that they could as well enjoy rides on a London omnibus, but Margaret knew the importance for a child of being able to fish and sail and ride. Richard, Mair, and the newest arrivals, Olwen and Gwilym, were brought up on a diet of simple, wholesome country food. Used as she was to home-baked oatcakes and freshly-caught river trout, Margaret despised the 'insipid' food most Londoners were forced to eat.

Increasingly also, Margaret was becoming involved in local politics. Quickly, she learnt to nurse the constituency for her husband. Lloyd George was not a good constituency MP. He was inspired by grand ideas but he loathed troublesome details. Besides, he had a pathological hatred of opening letters. By the interest she took, Margaret helped to mitigate much of the resentment which would otherwise have been felt among the Welsh. Mindful of this, Lloyd George encouraged her. 'You must make a good speech . . . That will surprise them,' he wrote in December 1895. 'I am sure you can do it,' he added. 'You have any quantity of brains of a very good quality if you only set them to work. THINK – that is what you must do.' Of course he was right. Margaret turned out to be a naturally gifted public speaker and a real source of influence within her orbit in Wales.

But now a train of events drew her away from Wales and up to London. In 1896 rumours began to circulate linking Lloyd George with a particularly messy and bitterly-fought divorce. There was even a 'confession', signed by a Mrs Catherine Edwards, swearing that Lloyd George was her lover and the father of her expected child. Fortunately, he was never called into the witness box; at the preliminary hearing he was referred to simply by the initials, A.B. The lawyers seem to have gone to great pains to make sure his reputation went unscathed, and in time Mrs Edwards withdrew her 'confession'. But Lloyd George had had a narrow escape and he knew it. He was probably not the child's father but only through luck. Almost certainly, he had slept with Mrs Edwards. 'If everything I have done . . . had got out,' he later told Oswald Mosley, 'I would have had to retire from politics.' Somewhat subdued, he wrote an apparently casual but telling letter to his wife: 'I know you would stick up for me on all occasions . . . I would trust you with my life.'

For all the promises to reform Lloyd George always made in the heat of the moment, he could never resist an attractive – and willing – woman. Before very long he was embroiled with another one, 'Mrs Tim' Davies, a talkative, over-dressed Putney housewife, who, according to Lloyd George's son, Richard, 'wore a fragrance like a basket of carnations'. In fact, it was Richard with his innocent, childish prattle who first aroused his mother to what was happening. Bitterly she reproached Lloyd George for falling by the wayside so soon. 'This business comes between you and me more so than you imagine, and is growing, and you know it and yet you cannot shake it off. It pains me to the quick and I am very unhappy. If you must go on as at present I don't know where it will end . . . Beware, don't give place for any scandal for the sake of your own personal self and your bright career.'

Lloyd George's reaction was fierce. He was swift to justify himself. 'Your letter this morning made me wild. There was the same self-complacent Pharisaism about it as ever . . . Be candid with yourself . . . and reflect whether you have not rather neglected your husband . . .

I have scores of times come home in the dead of night to a cold dark and comfortless flat . . . You have been a good mother. You have not – and I say this now not in anger – not always been a good wife.' He really meant it. 'Mrs Tim's' particular attraction was that she created a comfortable refuge for him in London. 'The idea . . .' spluttered Margaret, on her own admission, 'a prey to the green-eyed monster'. 'She [Mrs Tim] thinks you ought to be at her beck and call.' This time enough was enough. Margaret had learned her lesson. Swiftly she came up from Wales with the children and at the end of 1899, Lloyd George moved into his first real London home. It had taken ten years and much heartbreak for Margaret to adapt and bring about this compromise. In return she had the satisfaction of seeing the affair with 'Mrs Tim' peter out.

The house the Lloyd Georges moved into was a stone's throw away from Wandsworth Common, so that Margaret could preserve the illusion of being near the country and in the fresh air. It was an extraordinary household. 'Once you were over the threshold,' commented her son, 'you were in Wales.' It was true that no English was spoken; all the servants were not only Welsh but from Criccieth. If she had had her way, Margaret would no doubt have chosen them from the same street. Even when the house needed painting, the Criccieth house-painter was sent for. He and his assistant lived with the family for well over a week, sharing meals and swopping gossip from home. After that there was an endless procession of dressmakers, furniture restorers and shoemakers, whose train fares would be paid all the way from Wales and back. The one discrepancy in this home from home that Margaret had created was the fact that her children were being educated in English schools. To counteract this 'foreign' influence, she called in Lloyd George. Every night at the children's bedtime, he told them a story in Welsh from Scott or Dumas, taking pains – in order to make it a serial – to stop at the most exciting part. Then there were evenings of hymn-singing and frequent recitations of Welsh poetry. Such occasions were the most sophisticated entertainment the Lloyd Georges could offer at this stage.

In fact, even when Lloyd George became Prime Minister, there was no pandering to luxury. As in Lady John Russell's household, visitors were shocked at the sparse and simple food. Till quite late on, cider and lemonade were the only beverages served at table and Lloyd George would have to connive with the servants in order to send glasses of whisky up to his guests' rooms. As with his lapses in chapel attendance, he went to great lengths to hide this from Margaret. In some ways she maintained a great hold over him. It was a long time, for example, before he dared to play Sunday golf.

The lynchpin of the Wandsworth household was Sarah Jones, the indomitable Welsh housekeeper who was with Margaret for over forty years from 1900 till the day she died. When she first arrived in Wandsworth she was amazed and awed by the 'fancy' kitchen, but she soon settled down to cooking Lloyd George his favourite food – frizzled bacon, beans and fried potatoes for breakfast, lunch and high tea. Margaret herself had her hands full with the often impossible demands of her husband. He would read himself to sleep at 9 o'clock with 'Wild West' adventure stories but by 4.30 a.m. he would be awake and at 7 a.m. he was calling for the newspapers before breakfast, the main working period of his day. Sarah and Margaret never knew how many guests to expect: members of the Irish lobby movement, journalists and Labour MPs mingled with the Welsh 'regulars'. The immediate responsibility was mostly Sarah's for Margaret hated cooking, but later she was forced to juggle with the extra demands on the still-precarious family budget. Whatever she was doing, Lloyd George felt free peremptorily to interrupt her. 'Maggie bach!' he would shout and she would come running in from the garden or from upstairs, to find his tie or unearth a book or search for one of the thousand articles he managed to lose each day. At other times, for ever physically clumsy, he would be unable to open a door and would stand impatiently rattling the handle until Margaret or one of the servants rushed to the spot.

However, Margaret still found some time for the particular tasks which had given her pleasure in Wales. Although she would not sew and was bored by humdrum domestic work, she would devote a whole day to something extraordinary like preparing and smoking bacon. The garden, small as it was, became her particular domain where she grew roses and hyacinths and cherries, her favourite fruit. In the summer she was often to be seen in a shapeless old gardening dress and a floppy hat, at the top of a ladder, cramming cherries into her mouth.

Needless to say, society looked askance at this oddly-dressed figure, with the ruddy cheeks of a country-woman and no interest in fashionable ways. But the ordinary people loved her, for she was even more egalitarian than Lloyd George, who, although he did not mix easily with London society, liked the pace and dazzle of city life. Margaret was always more at home with 'the cottage man'. Especially liked was her impish sense of humour, for even on more or less formal occasions she would play practical jokes. She once put a rubber cushion that squeaked under an unsuspecting guest's chair seat.

And she had courage, a courage that was to be sorely tested as Lloyd George became more and more unpopular over his support for the Dutch settlers in the Boer War. In 1900, in the so-called 'Khaki election', a blazing, paraffin-soaked rag was thrown into his carriage. It landed straight in Margaret's lap. Lloyd George had to pick it up bare-handed and throw it out, then beat the sparks out of his wife's smouldering dress. This was in Bangor. In England he was more hated still, and jeers, rotten eggs and sometimes even stones greeted every public appearance. Margaret bore it all stoically, even when her son was victimized at school, and the Lloyd George legal practice, their financial lifeline, was in danger of closing down. Nevertheless, she often feared for Lloyd George's life. At Birmingham he was nearly lynched by a bloodthirsty mob who killed a policeman and smashed a telegraph pole in the mêlée. At first it was not known if Lloyd George had escaped and for four hours Margaret waited in agonized suspense to hear that he was safe. A few days later he appeared in public again – and with his wife's full support in spite of her fears.

In 1905 Lloyd George's persistence bore fruit when the Liberal party finally came to power. After fifteen years as a backbencher he was offered a post under Sir Henry Campbell-Bannerman as President of the Board of Trade. He was delighted, but while his political success now seemed assured, his family's happiness was about to be shattered by a cruel blow. In 1907, Margaret had to break to him terrible news – Mair, their placid, pretty eldest daughter had died of appendicitis in Wandsworth, aged only seventeen. To make matters worse, the death could have been prevented; she had hidden her pain because of some forthcoming exams. By the time the doctor was called, the appendix had ruptured and it was too late. For a few weeks Lloyd George was a broken man. It was left to Margaret to pick up the pieces of his life. She it was who arranged for him to go away while she sold the Wandsworth house and moved into one in Cheyne Walk where there would be no tormenting memories. Dry-eyed and with her courage and bearing still intact, it was she who played the part of a man; Lloyd George who wept on her shoulder. Later, Frances Stevenson, Lloyd George's long-term mistress, was to allege that secretly he blamed and hated his wife for Mair's death. If so, it was not evident, especially in these first faltering weeks when he leant on Margaret and depended on her for his very survival. Even a year later, in 1908, when Asquith appointed him Chancellor of the Exchequer, Lloyd George's reaction was to take a walk in the rain, crying for Mair who had not lived to see his triumph.

The family now moved into the Chancellor's official home, Number 11, Downing Street, where they were to remain till 1916. It was an unwieldy house with a labyrinth of passages at the rear, the result of 'improvements' by previous tenants. Even so, Margaret always preferred it to Number 10 – even after Margot Asquith's facelift. With its comfortable bedrooms and cosy sitting-room on the first floor, Number 11 could look quite homely by the light of its new gas-filled electric bulbs.

Both households needed policing day and night for the suffragettes had made Downing Street one of their prime targets for attack. Mostly, the clashes were humorous, for Lloyd George was a supporter of women's votes. But Margaret was fervently anti-feminist even before the bomb explosion in 1912 which ruined the inside of her linen closet. More independent than most women of her time, and one of the few to be an accomplished public speaker, something in her deeply conservative Welsh nature nevertheless recoiled at any change in the old ways.

This was one of the happiest periods in her married life. As Chancellor, Lloyd George was deeply involved in the 1909 'People's Budget'. The debate in the Commons raged fiercely for 73 days and several nights, and often

Lloyd George would look up wearily from the despatch-box to see Margaret watching from the Ladies' Gallery; behind the iron grille, that 'relic of the Dark Ages' which she so rightly scorned. Afterwards, in the early hours, they would walk home together across Whitehall. She was reconciled to his life in politics now.

She was not, however, reconciled to his penchant for other women, which in 1909 resulted in a further scandal. On 12 March 1909, the Chancellor of the Exchequer of England confronted *The People* newspaper in an unsavoury libel case. Rumours abounded that Margaret had finally left him and gone to Criccieth. In fact, braving the scandal, she was in the courtroom by his side. Her son says, in an admittedly biased biography, that she had ceased to believe his blundering protestations of innocence. Nor was she impressed by his plea that, 'One day I shall be Prime Minister . . . If you help me, you shall never regret your decision.' The only thing that saved her husband was his real and frightened vulnerability. Margaret could never, she said, resist him when he humbled his voice to plead, 'You must stand by me, Maggie. Otherwise, it's all over with me . . .' So, not for the last time, her rare generosity and protective loyalty sheltered him from the consequences of his own recklessness. Without her support, he might well have found the public far less ready to forgive him, especially in the restrictive moral climate of the time.

Lloyd George repaid his wife by falling in love again, this time with the woman who, after Margaret's death, was to become his second wife. Frances Stevenson was twenty-two years younger than Margaret, a mere twenty-three to Lloyd George's forty-eight. Modest and conventional in upbringing, she was nothing like the contemporary picture of a mistress as a 'fallen woman'. In fact, Lloyd George first saw in her a potential governess for his youngest daughter, Megan. In 1911, Frances

Stevenson spent the summer with the family at Criccieth. Secretly, she was already corresponding with Lloyd George: in fact, things had gone far enough for her to burn his letters. But her conscience still troubled her. She went to Scotland in an attempt to escape from it and there nearly married a reliable if somewhat dull civil servant. It was only Lloyd George's ruthlessness that won her back. He would stop at nothing. First, he won her sympathy by promising never to interfere in her life; next, he demanded her immediate return. Cunningly, for Frances was still young and naïve enough to be romantic about him, he presented her with Kitty O'Shea's *Life of Parnell*, whose career was ruined when he was cited in her divorce case. At least now Frances knew where she stood. It was to be a relationship 'on his own terms' or nothing. Eventually, as she was to do so many times, Frances capitulated and returned, nominally as his secretary, in 1912. 'Lloyd George,' she said later, 'became my life's vocation.'

For over thirty years Frances Stevenson had to be content with a hole-in-the-corner existence of back doors and deception, hidden away from the eyes of the world. Her hard work went largely unrewarded; her daughter by Lloyd George could never bear his name. It was far from the cosy, domestic idyll she was later to describe in her autobiography. The diary of A. J. Sylvester, Lloyd George's private secretary, has made this clear, bringing light to bear on what she dismissed as the 'lean' times in her life. Less able than Margaret to cope with Lloyd George's titanic fits of temper, she was often unhappy, frequently in tears. He would even turn on her after she had beaten him at golf. Whereas he respected Margaret for standing up to him – 'She is the best of the bunch . . . when we were on the point of having a frightful row she stepped in and said, "I will have none of it," ' – to Frances he could be gratuitously cruel. Once, several years later, when he became absurdly jealous, he held her down by force till she confessed to some imaginary act of infidelity. No wonder she was often ill with the strain.

Then there was Margaret herself, still very much in evidence and surrounded by a devoted family who fiercely took her part. Megan, Lloyd George's special favourite, openly showed her dislike of Frances and did her best to woo her father away from his mistress's side. Sylvester's diary shows that husband and wife were closer than Frances Stevenson liked to admit. 'You talk as if my affection for you came and went,' Lloyd George wrote to Margaret. 'No more than the sea does because the tide ebbs and flows. There is just as much water in it . . .' Lloyd George could never hope to escape from the past that he shared with Margaret, nor was it in him to want to: she was an essential part of his life, bringing him a comfort and security that the younger woman could never supply. Significantly, whereas Frances in her diary called herself 'married', Lloyd George looked on her as taking the place of Mair, 'my little girl whom I lost . . .' It was unthinkable that he would ever divorce Margaret as Frances once claimed he was about to do. Sylvester, who knew him well, completely discounted any such possibility – although admitting that this was something Lloyd George might not have wished Frances to know.

In any case, Margaret's personal struggles now became submerged in a far greater conflict. In 1915, a year after the outbreak of war, Lloyd George became Minister of Munitions. Then developed a quarrel over the conduct of the war between Lloyd George and Asquith, for Asquith, although clever and conscientious, was neither a decisive nor an inspiring war leader. In 1916 Asquith resigned, never imagining that Lloyd George would be able to form a government. He could and did, bracing himself to lead the country through a gruelling war.

Behind this change of ministry lay two years of bitter political in-fighting, with Mrs Asquith, according to Frances Stevenson, 'quite mad . . . rushing all over the place sending messages to people. She is most abusive about D., and cannot think of things bad enough to say about him.' Margaret, who had never been particularly ambitious, was largely oblivious to it all and graciously told the Asquiths to take their time in moving from Number 10. 'We will soon be moving in again, in any case,' was Margot Asquith's tart reply. However, Lloyd George got his own back by comparing his wife's war-work with her predecessor's. 'Downing Street was never put to as good use,' he declared. 'Heavens! What a contrast to [Mrs Asquith]. Isn't she making a fine exhibition of herself in her autobiography?'

Certainly, Number 10 saw no more brilliant dinner parties. Instead, Margaret filled it with Welsh expatriates, all busy knitting scarves and socks and making clothes for the Comforts Fund for Welsh Troops. In all, £200,000 was collected, and though little went to the unfortunate Scots or English, Margaret was created a Dame after the Paris Peace Conference in 1919. Another tribute came from an unknown admirer. On Armistice Day, 11 November 1919, a parcel was delivered to Number 10. Inside was a diamond and sapphire bracelet and a note: 'To the Wife of the Man who Won the War.'

In many ways she deserved it. She did much in those years to shield Lloyd George from unnecessary anxiety. He slept badly as it was, dreaming of the young men he was sending to their deaths. Margaret learned to discern what he was thinking by listening to the footsteps in his study. When things looked hopeful, or he was pleased with a phrase in one of his speeches, he hopped nimbly around, almost dancing. When he was oppressed and overcome by worry, he walked up and down with slow, deliberate steps. Then she would send all but the most important visitors away. Often, too, she would have to reassure him about their two sons fighting in the trenches, particularly when he became morbidly convinced that Dick, the eldest one, was dead. 'Mrs L.G. is as brave as a lion,' wrote Lord Riddell, a friend. Not surprisingly, she struck up a great friendship with the young Winston Churchill, who saw in her, 'all that was most strong and true in the British race'. Margaret, for her part, admitted that she rather liked the idea of him acting as a thorn in the side of her husband, just as Lloyd George had done to his party leader, Gladstone.

Meanwhile, life in Number 10 was as spartan as ever. An unexpected guest recalling dinner there, wrote in 1917: 'So far as the food, service and appointments were concerned, it looked as if a small suburban household were picknicking in Downing Street – the same simple food, the same little domestic servant, the same mixture of tea and dinner.'

In 1922, the wartime coalition that Lloyd George's Liberals had formed with the Conservatives collapsed when the Tories decided to fight the election alone. At the age of fifty-nine and after seventeen years in the Cabinet, Lloyd George finally quit office. He did not dream it possible at the time, but he would never again be a minister. The eighteen years left to him in parliament were spent in the wilderness trying to get back. He sat on committees, drew up policies, wrote endless newspaper articles, travelled widely and met heads of state. Sylvester says that privately his wife, at any rate, knew it was in vain. 'Whatever happens,' she consoled a distraught Megan, 'Tada [Lloyd George] will be the power. He will be tremendous in opposition . . .' But now, good-humouredly, she set about the mammoth job of packing. 'The mess is indescribable . . . The general election will be a rest after this . . . books, papers, photos, caskets, overflowing wastepaper baskets, men in aprons, depressed messengers abound . . . Newnham [Lloyd George's valet] walks about with the air of a man whose sufferings are intense . . .'

When they left Downing Street the Lloyd Georges had two homes to go to. Later they acquired another in London for their mutual use. For the moment, Lloyd George lived mostly at Churt in Surrey in a house called *Bron-y-de* (Bosom of the South) he had built the year before. Frances had chosen the site, much to Margaret's disgust. 'The only part of the house facing *de* (south) is the front door,' she observed scathingly. 'The dining room, drawing room and all good bedrooms face north west, so *pen ol* (behind) and not *bron* (breast) is the best name for it.' South-facing or not, Margaret was a regular visitor and whenever she arrived, Frances had to leave – sometimes, as Sylvester recalled, in a hurry, by the back door. If she stayed she faced the even more humiliating prospect of eating with the children in the nursery, or in her bedroom alone. Naturally, when Margaret was not there, Frances lived with Lloyd George quite openly, although she was also employed in a real capacity as his secretary. It was only after Frances's arrival that his letters and papers were properly documented. Sylvester gives her all due credit for this, but points out that, while she probably knew more than Margaret about the day-to-day running of Lloyd George's affairs, Frances had no scope for political influence. Megan, if anyone, was Lloyd George's confidante here.

The situation with Frances, coupled with Margaret's pride and her natural indolence, led her once again to seek the seclusion of Wales. For £2000 she had built a house in Criccieth and called it *Brynawelon*, Hill of the Breezes. It was an ugly, sprawling Edwardian house – Lord Riddell likened it to the 'villa of a prosperous tradesman' – but she surrounded it with a glorious garden. Once a year she would disappear under a deluge of seed catalogues and then re-emerge to plant what she had ordered herself. She would even snip shoots off bouquets presented to her and grow them in a pot.

Lloyd George, Sylvester says, visited her quite frequently, unceremoniously 'depositing' Frances. He once even used the excuse that, if he did not go, Margaret would come to him immediately, although it was Christmas, an unlikely time for her to think of leaving Wales. There was an affectionate, half-teasing, half-grumbling ceremonial about his visits which Margaret understood well. She had the same sense of humour. He would start by complaining about the Welsh weather: 'I know of no place where it rains so incessantly . . . If you wish to see an eclipse at any time, go to Criccieth.' When he arrived Margaret sometimes dressed the family in fancy-dress to surprise him – there was an element of fantasy in both their ideas of humour. They would spin the tallest of tall stories. 'Goodness!' Margaret would say, pretending to peer into the far, far distance, 'I can see St David's Head.' As this was eighty miles from Criccieth, it was hardly likely but Lloyd George would pick up his cue immediately.

'You're right,' he would retort, 'and there's Gwilym [their son] on the side of the hill.'

'Gwilym?' came the reply, then after much shading of the eyes, 'Oh, yes.'

Lloyd George usually had the last word and this time was no different. 'It's Gwilym,' he affirmed. 'One of his fly-buttons is unfastened.' He found this companionable badinage both restful and enjoyable. Frances Stevenson, for all her devotion, was a serious young woman.

To keep him happy, Lloyd George needed a lot of entertaining. Games of golf were organized and family picnics by the river. There was a notorious dawn foray up Snowdon to see the sunrise when all they saw, all around them, was mist. More successful were the evening sing-songs on the beach after chapel. Lloyd George prided himself on his rendering of Welsh hymns. 'I feel that it is good for me to come down here . . . to the simple life,' he wrote after a week or so in which family, servants and secretaries had endlessly scurried around.

In 1928 Margaret's influence secured for Megan the Liberal nomination for Anglesey. Lloyd George wrote to congratulate 'the little M' and commended 'the big M' on her speech, which went straight to the point, like those known at the bar as 'good verdict getters'. 'In Wales . . . she is loved, admired and is the uncrowned queen,' commented Sylvester, while a party spokesman noted approvingly: 'Her simple, direct ways appeal to the people.' With Margaret's help, Megan was returned with ease, bringing the number of Lloyd Georges in the House up to three – Gwilym had been MP for Pembrokeshire since 1922.

Margaret had always jealously guarded the Caernarvon Boroughs seat, but now her interest spread to encompass all the Liberal constituencies in Wales. In 1921 she had made fifty-eight speeches in fourteen days while campaigning for Ernest Evans, Lloyd George's secretary, in a crucial by-election. In the recent general elections, her programme had been equally arduous, for Lloyd George was needed to lead the campaign in the rest of the country, leaving Margaret to rally Liberal Wales. Yet Margaret continued to be surprisingly unpolitical. The decisions of the Criccieth Urban District Council, of which she was chairman, had always seemed more real to her than world affairs. While Lloyd George and Megan discussed complex international questions, she would listen with what Megan called her 'knitting-face', using the time to file her husband's nails. Nevertheless, Liberal victories, even Lloyd George victories in Wales, were never foregone conclusions, and when Lloyd

George won – even in 1931 as an *independent* Liberal – it was a personal victory for her. Four years after Margaret's death, Lloyd George resigned and Caernarvon Boroughs went back to what it had been before – a Tory seat.

Margaret's campaign successes were all the more remarkable in view of Lloyd George's growing unpopularity. His affair with Frances Stevenson and the birth of her daughter, Jennifer, in 1929, had, in the areas where they were common knowledge, taken their toll. To this day, it has never been proved that Lloyd George was definitely the father, but at the time even the rumours were damaging enough. Yet, ironically, by this stage, Lloyd George's relationship with his mistress was far from flourishing. In her early forties Frances Stevenson had fallen passionately in love with another man – Colonel Thomas Tweed, head of Lloyd George's political office. He and not Lloyd George was the great love of her middle years, although not surprisingly he goes unmentioned in her autobiography, written as Countess Lloyd George. Lloyd George did not suspect until he was told by his wife, who derived an understandable satisfaction from travelling to Churt and giving him the news herself. She had learnt of the affair from the Welsh maid in Frances's flat.

In time, the storm blew over although Lloyd George felt betrayed enough never to trust Frances entirely again. Nor did he trust Tweed, but he could not sack him from his post. As a colleague he knew too much about the dubious Lloyd George Political Fund, 'a quarter of a million of [Liberal] money', according to Sylvester, which he believed Lloyd George was trying to ear-mark for his personal use. That, too, was to create a scandal. By 1937 Frances, Jennifer and Lloyd George were seen together in public enough for questions to be asked about his 'second family'. Hastily Frances adopted Jennifer officially in 1938. But the gossip enraged Lloyd George . . . 'Like Samson, I will pull down the pillars to kill the Philistines, even if I am overwhelmed . . . I will meet anybody in the Caernarvon Boroughs. I will guarantee they won't kick me out there. The old girl will stand by me.' The 'old girl' indeed arranged a special showing of holiday films, to show the audience and the world what a close family they were. She may or may not have known that films existed of Frances in the very same spot, holidaying with Lloyd George before his family arrived.

There were happy times, too, abroad for Margaret. She sailed with Lloyd George all over the world. But she could happily return from staying at the White House, to Criccieth, where she rose early each morning to feed her flock of scrawny hens. She was too soft-hearted ever to kill them to eat: they were allowed to roam free in the gardens, scratching the lawn and pecking at the plants until they died peacefully of advanced old age. One trip Margaret remembered with especial pleasure. In 1938 Lloyd George took her to the South of France to celebrate their golden wedding. At a luncheon in the Carlton Hotel, Cannes, they were joined by Winston Churchill, who proposed the toast, drunk in champagne in a silver-gilt loving-cup. A month later in Wales at a public ceremony to mark the occasion, Lloyd George paid a humorous tribute to his wife. 'Marriage,' he began, 'is the greatest and oldest partnership in the world . . . the best and truest friendship . . . I need hardly say,' he continued, 'that my wife and I are of different temperaments. One is contentious, combative, and stormy. That is my wife. Then, there is the other partner, placid, calm, peaceful and patient. That is me.' His fellow-countrymen knew the truth well enough to laugh loud and long.

When the Second World War broke, Margaret was at Criccieth, and was joined there before long by her husband. Lloyd George had been asked to be a part of Churchill's cabinet but he was old now – seventy-six – and ailing and embittered by his quarrel with Neville Chamberlain. He refused to serve alongside Chamberlain even in war. He had never been a physical coward – like Margaret, he had always revelled in storms at sea – but the air raids over Churt began to obsess and terrify him. 'If I stay here it will kill me,' he said to Frances, and retired, 'shaking and doddering' to his wife in Wales. The £6000 luxury air-raid shelter at Churt, sixty feet below ground with electric light, stocks of food, and non-inflammable furniture, was hardly used. Instead, Lloyd George began to build another one at Brynawelon.

But he was not at Criccieth in November 1940, when Margaret slipped at a neighbour's house on the highly-polished parquet floor. An X-ray revealed a cracked hip-bone but it was not thought serious, even at her age of seventy-five. She was only expected to be in bed for a few weeks, and Lloyd George did not bother to come down. But by January 1941, the leg was no nearer healing; rather, Margaret became feverish and drowsy, her pulse fast and weak. Her horrified family saw her slipping away before their eyes. In a severe snowstorm, Lloyd George set off by car to be with her, having previously contacted the King's doctor, Lord Dawson of Penn. Neither of them reached Criccieth in time. At 10.20 on the morning of 20 January, Margaret died. At the time Lloyd George was marooned in a village some way off; his car had had to be dug out of a snowdrift by the villagers the previous night. Sobbing, he heard the news over the telephone. 'She was a great old pal.' When he eventually reached Brynawelon, he looked old and tired. He was wearing a woollen scarf for the first time in his life. Sylvester noted later that this marked the start of his own decline.

Even in the austerity of wartime the flowers for

Margaret's funeral were so numerous that enormous bunches had to be stuck into the ten foot snowdrifts outside the house. The tiny post office was swamped with telegrams from all over the world. The local people, Margaret's friends, showed their feelings by their practical help. Butter, milk, sides of bacon, joints of beef poured in from the neighbouring farms to feed the guests at the funeral. Of all the tributes paid to her, it was the one Margaret would have treasured most. 'She was still after all those crowded and splendid years,' said a friend, 'an Eifionydd housewife . . . She had never been dazzled, she had never lost her head . . . for her there was always the age-old background of the Eifionydd life. That was her anchor in the storms and calms of fifty years of politics.' If she needed an anchor, she supplied one too. Lloyd George used her as an anchor and her home as his refuge, to the end of their married life.

Bibliography

GENERAL

Iremonger, Lucille: *And His Charming Lady*, 1961
Iremonger, Lucille: *The Fiery Chariot*, 1970
Lee, Elizabeth: *Wives of the Prime Ministers*, 1918
Van Thal, Herbert (ed.): *The Prime Ministers*, Volume I, 1974, Volume II, 1975

CHAPTER ONE: LADY CHATHAM

Annan, Noel: *Roxburgh of Stowe*, 1966
Edwards, E. A. (ed.): *The Love Letters of William Pitt, First Lord Chatham*, 1926
Guedalla, Philip (ed.): Macaulay's *Second Essay on William Pitt, Earl of Chatham (1844)*, 1913
Lever, Sir Tresham: *The House of Pitt*, 1947
Plumb, J. H.: *Chatham*, 1953
Rosebery, Lord: *Chatham, His Early Life and Connections*, 1910
Sherrard, O. A.: *Lord Chatham, A War Minister in the Making*, 1952; *Lord Chatham, Pitt and the Seven Years' War*, 1955; *Lord Chatham and America*, 1958
Williams, Basil: *The Life of William Pitt, Earl of Chatham*, Volume I, 1913, Volume II, 1915

CHAPTER TWO: LADY PEEL

Cardwell, E. (ed. with Lord Mahon): *Memoirs of Rt. Hon. Sir Robert Peel*, 1856
Clark, George S. R. K.: *Peel*, 1936
Edgcumbe, R. (ed.): *Diary of Frances, Lady Shelley*, 1912
Gash, Norman: *Mr Secretary Peel*, 1961; *Sir Robert Peel*, 1972
Lever, Sir Tresham: *The Life and Times of Sir Robert Peel*, 1942
Parker, C. S. (ed.): *Sir Robert Peel from his Private Papers*, 1899
Peel, George (ed.): *The Private Letters of Sir Robert Peel*, 1920
Ramsay, A. A. W.: *Sir Robert Peel*, 1928

CHAPTER THREE: LADY PALMERSTON

Airlie, Countess of: *Lady Palmerston and her Times*, 1922; *In Whig Society*, 1921
Ashley, Hon. Evelyn: *The Life of Henry John, Viscount Palmerston*, 1876
Bailey, F. E.: *The Love Story of Lady Palmerston*, 1938
Baring Pemberton, W.: *Lord Palmerston*, 1926
Cecil, David: *The Young Melbourne*, 1939
Guedalla, Philip: *Palmerston*, 1926
Hayward, Abraham: *Lady Palmerston, A Biographical Sketch*, (Reprinted by permission from *The Times* of September 15, 1869)
Lever, Tresham: *The Letters of Lady Palmerston*, 1957
Ridley, Jasper: *Lord Palmerston*, 1970

CHAPTER FOUR: LADY JOHN RUSSELL

Champneys, Basil: *The Life of Adelaide Drummond*, 1915
Gooch, G. P. (ed.): *Lord John Russell: Later Correspondence* 1925
Peel, Lady Georgiana: *Recollections*, 1920
Prest, John: *John, Earl Russell*, 1972
Russell, Lady Agatha: *Lady John Russell: A Memoir*, 1910
Russell, Bertrand and Patricia (ed.): *The Amberley Papers*, 1937

Russell, Rollo (ed.): *Lord John Russell: Early Correspondence*, 1913
Walpole, Sir Spencer: *The Life of Lord John Russell*, 1889

CHAPTER FIVE: MRS DISRAELI

Blake, Robert: *Disraeli*, 1966
Elletson, D. H.: *Maryannery: Mrs Lincoln and Mrs Disraeli*, 1959
Hardwick, Mollie: *Mrs Dizzy*, 1972
Maurois, André: *Disraeli: A Picture of the Victorian Age*, 1927
Pearson, Hesketh: *Dizzy*, 1951
Sykes, James: *Mary Anne Disraeli*, 1928

CHAPTER SIX: MRS GLADSTONE

Battiscombe, Georgina: *Mrs Gladstone: The Portrait of a Marriage*, 1956
Checkland, S. G.: *The Gladstones: A Family Biography*, 1971
Drew, Mary: *Catherine Gladstone*, 1919
Magnus, Philip: *Gladstone, A Biography*, 1963
Morley, John: *The Life of William Ewart Gladstone*, 1903
Pratt, Edwin: *Catherine Gladstone*, 1898

CHAPTER SEVEN: MRS ASQUITH

Asquith, Lady Cynthia: *Diaries 1915–18*, 1968
Asquith, H. H.: *Memories and Reflections*, 1928
Asquith, Margot: *Autobiography*, *Volume One*, 1920, *Volume Two*, 1922
Asquith, Margot: *More Memories*, 1933
Asquith, Margot: *Off the Record*, 1943
Bonham-Carter, Mark: *Introduction* to Margot Asquith's *Autobiography*, new edition, 1962
Crathorne, Nancy: *Tennant's Stalk, the story of The Tennants of the Glen*, 1973
Jenkins, Roy: *Asquith*, 1964
Minney, R. J.: *'Puffin' Asquith*, 1973
Sykes, Christopher: *Nancy, the Life of Lady Astor*, 1972

CHAPTER EIGHT: DAME MARGARET LLOYD GEORGE

Cross, Colin (ed.): *Life with Lloyd George, The Diary of A. J. Sylvester*, 1975

Edwards, J. Hugh: *David Lloyd George: the Man and the Statesman*, 1913

George, William: *My Brother and I*, 1958

Grigg, John: *The Young Lloyd George*, 1975

Gwynedd, Viscount: *Dame Margaret*, 1947

Lloyd-George, Earl: *Lloyd George*, 1960

Lloyd-George, Frances, Countess: *The Years That Are Past*, 1967

Morgan, Kenneth (ed.): *David Lloyd George, Family Letters*, 1973

Owen, Frank: *Tempestuous Journey, Lloyd George His Life and Times*, 1954

Sylvester, A. J.: *The Real Lloyd George*, 1947

Taylor, A. J. P. (ed.): *Frances Stevenson, A Diary*, 1971

Index